So What Did You Expect?

So What Did You Expect?

A MEMOIR

ANTHONY SHAFFER

PICADOR

First published 2001 by Picador
an imprint of Pan Macmillan Ltd
Pan Macmillan, 20 New Wharf Road, London N1 9RR
Basingstoke and Oxford
Associated companies throughout the world
www.panmacmillan.com

ISBN 0 330 39043 0

Copyright © Anthony Shaffer 2001

1 3 5 7 9 8 6 4 2

A CIP catalogue record for this book is available from
the British Library.

Typeset by SetSystems Ltd, Saffron Walden, Essex
Printed and bound in Great Britain by
Mackays of Chatham plc, Chatham, Kent

This book is dedicated to the ladies in my life – progenital or amatory – to whose loving ministrations I mostly owe the joyful satisfactions in it; and also to the many painstaking labours which I often think contain my best work, and which for many disparate, and desperate reasons were never realized, and became my unjoyful dissatisfactions.

'A memoir is how one remembers one's own life, while an autobiography is history, requiring research, dates, facts double-checked . . . After all, one's recollected life is just about all that's left at the end of the day when the work is done, and gone, property now of others.'

GORE VIDAL, *Palimpsest*

Contents

So What Did You Expect?

Acknowledgements

While these memoirs have been a labour of love, I hope to continue for a few more bountiful years, to have some more warmed by the often-expressed love of my extraordinary living wives, both current and past, Diane and Carolyn, and of my children, Claudia and Cressida. Claudia, somewhat unsung in this memoir, won the best scholarship of her year to Cambridge, electing to go to Sidney Sussex on the eccentric grounds that their most famous old boy was Oliver Cromwell, and later became head of her department at the prestigious literary agency, Curtis Brown; she also made this book possible with her brilliant new-age IT skills (as did also the technical wizardry and fine aesthetic judgement of the ineluctable Marie Jo Capece Minutolo). Cressida, although stricken by an almost terminal case of diabetes, has struggled courageously back to health with the help of many loathsome self-inflicted stomach injections and her recently found house in the beautiful valleys of Wales; she promises a remarkable life in sculpting.

And also, of course, my handsome and hugely talented stepson Jason Connery and his wife Mia, and their young son, my quasi-grandson, Dashiell. Jason, who, completely besotted, behaves towards this infant prodigy as if he were the first man ever to have fathered a child, which compensates him for his current battle for roles and recognition in Hollywood after a career which started with a most beguiling TV *Robin Hood* series for Harlech and continued with quite marvellous performances in the First World War play *Journey's End* and a so-far unreleased film of *Macbeth*, in which he speaks the verse just about as well as it has ever been done. I must apologize for the somewhat skinny references to him and his young family in these pages.

And of course there are my brothers Peter and Brian. The former, though increasingly perplexed by modern mores and electronic computerized writing mechanical techniques, is as inventive and commanding as ever, scouring the shops for early steam-portable typewriters. He has, I suppose achieved the status of pre-eminent British playwright – a position which, in my opinion, he shares with Tom Stoppard. The two, needless to say, are close friends, and greatly admire each other's work, and are now both knights, Peter having been so dubbed on 18 May this year.

The extent of this approbation is best exemplified by Peter's most gratified anecdote about Tom. In 1974, after the first night of *Equus*, Stoppard was descending the stairs of the theatre as Peter was ascending them. He turned briefly to Peter, pronounced the one word 'Cunt!' and marched on.

This, from the wittiest writer in the English language, was the most respectful accolade and was as such proudly and gleefully accepted. So what did he expect?

The latter, Brian, now himself over seventy and mysteriously without a grey hair in his head, rejoices with his arcane professorial American wife Nellan in the genius and joy of their children, Mark, after the briefest possible period of study now a doctor, and Milo, like his father one of the microscopic band of men ever to have been awarded a Fellowship of Trinity on the strength of their Tripos papers. This was to his father's rueful chagrin – his son was two weeks younger than when he had achieved it himself!

In addition I also have a satisfying number of loving friends, some of whom have appeared here and others who have modestly chosen to remain outside its covers or nameless within them.

And lastly I must mention one dear absent friend, my precious mother, who, alas before I could finish this book, died last year at the age of ninety-four, her life's work fully completed and mercifully in absolute possession of her formidable faculties, in no pain and fully prepared to go and join her husband, cherished through over fifty years of marriage.

So What Did You Expect?

1. Beginnings

The first nine years of my life were spent in Liverpool, where we lived at 55 Croxteth Road, near Sefton Park. My father had brought my mother there from Devonport, and he worked in the property business when he could spare time from his more favourite boulevardier activities of golf, bridge and snooker.

We went to school locally at Holly Lee – a fairly innocuous kindergarten loathed on sight by my twin brother Peter, whose immediate protest took the form of overturning his desk.

The first intimation of the difficulty of being a twin came to me in a favourite story of my mother's: apparently after I was born (on 15 May 1926, at 9.30 a.m., weighing six and a half pounds) Father, doctor and Grandmother, the latter putting me safely in a crib, all retired, leaving my mother alone with a single nurse.

To everyone's surprise and the mortification of the doctor, whose stethoscope had plainly failed to detect two heartbeats, a second baby was born at 9.35 a.m. My grandmother returned to the room and exclaimed in surprise, 'Who put the baby on the bed?' She then gasped with joyous amazement when she looked into the crib and realized that there were two babies. A gloomier view of the event was taken by my great-grandfather, whose advice was to 'lock the door and tell nobody'. In view of the lifetime's confusion that followed for Peter and myself, this was probably the soundest advice we could have been given.

Birth was followed by nine years of somewhat cosseted growing-up in a large house stocked with servants with laborious 1930s titles – housemaids, cooks-general, day and night nurses, gardeners and under-gardeners, chauffeurs and under-chauffeurs, ladies' maids and scullerymaids, most later to be replaced by the commanding and ubiquitous Nurse Murphy, a stout Irish bossy-boots.

From this fortress I remember seeing the lamplighter turning on the street gas lamps, and watching airships floating overhead, including the doomed *R101*, and hearing the cries of the muffin man delivering his goodies in time for tea, and the tinkling bells of the tramcars as they reached their terminal point and turned round at the end of the street, and the chants of the unemployed as they marched by. Perhaps most significantly of all for me, I recall hearing and reading (with difficulty) of William Herbert Wallace's arrest and conviction for the murder of his wife in a house in a nearby suburb. Her death occurred at a time when he could scarcely have done it, though, almost uniquely, he was released by the court of appeal.

We emerged from time to time to go to school or neighbouring Sefton Park, where we gazed at captive birds in a sad little aviary or played at pirates on a miniature galleon anchored on a small lake. Peter and I would be dressed in identically detested brown whipcord imported from Rowes of Bond Street, London. No matter how hard we rubbed the seats of the trousers with pumice stone or brick, they wouldn't wear out.

Our cultural life was not neglected and many eminent intellectuals came often to the house, along with musicians. I remember the famous pianist Benno Moisenwitsch tearing a pack of playing cards in half to demonstrate his finger strength. My parents weren't tremendously amused when I tried to emulate this feat, a fact they discovered at their next bridge evening (of county player standard, they didn't relish bifurcated playing cards).

We also were taken regularly to the Liverpool Playhouse. At the first performance I attended, incidentally the first play I ever saw, I watched Michael Redgrave in a children's play that I seem to remember he wrote himself called *The Green Arrow*. A gang of kidnappers whose calling card was a green arrow was on the loose, and our young heroes were strictly abjured that on no account whatsoever were they to leave the house. At the end of the first act, men arrived and told the children that they must come with them immediately as their parents were in grave danger. They obeyed, and left the house. The door slammed behind them – and pinned to it was the eponymous green arrow! Needless to say, the interval was spent in a fever of dread and apprehension wondering what fearful things were happening to our infant heroes.

This, I have always thought, was a seminal event. It stimulated a taste for the thriller, the melodrama and the suspense play, which have always seemed to me to be the ideal genres for storytelling. After all, you must be a pretty dull dog if you don't crucially want to know what happens next. If, for instance, you propose to someone that behind the door on stage is the most heart-stoppingly unspeakable creature ever conceived in the whole history of the universe, but as it starts to open he falls sound asleep, there is no story you can possibly tell him. Furthermore, under the umbrella of these forms, any message or philosophical disquisition – if that is your game – is possible. Suspense, whether a whodunnit or whydunnit or howdunnit, is merely the sugar coating on the pill; by the time you have swallowed it, the medicine has gone down, no matter what kind it may be.

Dramatic performances were not limited to the professional stage. At school we were invited to play the part of Shadows in the pantomime but I am afraid that neither Peter nor I was up to it. We found it quite impossible to learn the lines and despite elaborate home-made costumes and many painstaking rehearsals we were entirely insufficient. If Yat Malmgren (the famed gestural teacher) had seen us it might have suggested the name he later gave to certain overmelodramatic gestures – 'shadow moves'!

Childhood memories are of course dubious, and probably not as interesting or engaging as the author imagines. Nonetheless, here are a few disassociated ones culled from an incompetently Alzheimian brain.

Peter and I communicated in a secret language to the gratifying bafflement of our elders, who apparently spent hours eavesdropping outside our nursery door, trying to break the code. Alas neither my brother nor I can remember a single word of this language. Childhood is perhaps mercifully self-sealing.

At Holly Lee School, which we attended from nine to thirteen years old, a genial staff provided good soccer instruction. In my position on the field, outside right – the same as the revered Stanley Matthews – I once played for the school, rather dismally in fact, because I was marked by a huge Yugoslavian who cheerfully spent the afternoon running the studs on his boots up and down my calves unremarked by the referee.

Further blind eyes were turned to a primitive betting game played with cigarette cards that involved highly skilled flicking techniques to send your card spinning to the floor from the desktop to cover others already there. I remember I once had charge of the bank of cards overnight, and was severely tempted to steal from it, and did so, though I returned them the next morning. I think it must have been my first criminal impulse. Later it was to escalate to kleptomania in sweet shops and voyeurism in historically famous murder sites.

The teachers also provided compelling stories on Friday afternoons, often in serial form (perhaps a cunning device to ensure maximum school attendance).

I have almost convinced myself that it was I who persuaded my parents to move south when I was nine years old. 'We've served our apprenticeships in the provinces,' I said, 'let's bring the show in' – by 'in' I of course meant London. At least that was my remembrance of things, though I suspect that my mother would probably deny it today. At any rate it was to London we went, settling in Ferncroft Avenue, Hampstead, in a large double-fronted house with a billiard room, two staircases and a score of servants

Childhood continued in a preparatory school called the Hall under the tutelage of Mr Wathen, a chota-peggish sort of wallah, and his strange, crazed collection of ambivalently sexed masters, Mr Dodd, who covered your head with his gown before stuffing it into a locker; Mr Allen, with his electric board games for teaching Latin; Miss Duffay, with her refined ladies' maid manners and exquisite calligraphy; and the austere paedo-philic Mr Mallard, who I suspect was to have had such a profound effect on my brother Peter's sexual bias. I never did quite get to the bottom of this (no prurient snide amusement intended) – a veiled incident at a private tea party, I think – and we proceeded to share the uniquely close life of twins into our late teens, before the sexual penny dropped.

There were, of course, enough clues – dances avoided on double dates, literary references and preferences, anecdotes and questionable stories, etc., etc. It wasn't until by complete accident that, unobserved, I happened to witness late one night an amatory encounter on the steps of Earls Terrace in Kensington High Street that the matter of his sexual inclination was put beyond doubt.

Peter, of course, in those days, kept the matter very much to himself, even in his anguish going so far as to leave England and settle courageously in Hell's Kitchen, New York City – as the West mid-40s in Manhattan were called – finding employment with Doubleday Bookshops and the new York Public Library.

I visited him in the latter place once and I remember him showing me a first edition of *The Importance of Being Earnest* there, containing a fourth act where the Reverend Chasuble and Miss Prism become what is now called an item, which it certainly didn't need. He also gave me a tour of the building, pointing out various salient features, including a number of stone lions at the front entrance, which were said to roar every time a virgin passed by! An oldie and a goldie, I suspect.

I sometimes think that Peter would have been equally silent if he had not been born both homosexual and Jewish. It is a classic recipe for storytelling – particularly legendary storytelling. It's the best hideyhole in the world. Later he was to peer out at the world in his play *Yonadab*, a piece almost exclusively concerned with heterosexual voyeurism at the court of King David, a subject that could not conceivably interest him unless hidden in a biblical legend.

But I digress. I entered into the sporting and bullying life of the school enthusiastically, playing goalie in the yard, standing watchfully between two tall elms that surprisingly are still there, and targeting a boy called Stonehill, almost as tall but unfortunately for him totally uncoordinated, alternately executing him by pulling the pins out of an easel so that the blackboard fell like a guillotine, and gluing the seat of his trousers to his desk bench. I can't imagine what his mother must have thought as he returned night after night with it missing.

Almost as uncoordinated and certainly as unconvincing at sports was my brother Peter, whom they took great pains to hide in the outfield when playing cricket. Being an identical twin, I once deputized for him in a tennis final and won. How he ever got to the final in the first place must remain a mystery.

On the whole, prep-school passed pleasantly enough as we marched in a crocodile file through the streets of Hampstead, past the Q Theatre, playing at one time *I Killed the Count*, a wonderful mystery where everyone confessed to the murder so the detective could arrest no one (placing another signpost towards one's latter career), and past Swiss Cottage, to perform contemporary aerobics in the Finchley Road gym, rope-climbing and leaping over pommel-horses to Sousa marches boldly struck off on an appallingly out-of-tune upright piano by a parody of a severely eyeglassed spinster in mauve bombazine.

Eventually it was time to leave, and so happy had we been that we asked our parents if we could stay on another term. Quite surprisingly they acquiesced, and so it was arranged.

But the time was September 1939, and the world changed dramatically.

We were evacuated on an eccentric whim of my father's to Bognor Regis – just about as close to the German front line as you could get without learning the goosestep. In the process we had a spectacular view of the Battle of Britain, and also missed our places at Westminster, a school for which we had been put down at birth.

We now zigzagged across the country in a merry game of Hiding from the Hun, which took us to the bucolic loveliness of Cheltenham and the sterner realities of Blackpool Grammar School, and more extensively to King Edward VII at Lytham St Anne's. This move up north had been occasioned not, I suspect, to put further distance between us and the Wehrmacht, but by the fact that my father's mother still lived in Blackpool, as did his brother Percy, a lean, freckled man of questionable sanity. (He once shot the family dog with a Home Guard rifle by mistake while chasing his sister Lily with it.) Our education since the declaration of war had been conducted by a succession of tiresome tutors, along with our mother, whom I remember demonstrated a quite phenomenal grasp of Galilean astrophysics with the aid of an orange on a string to represent the sun.

Our eventual descent down south was inspired by our gaining scholarships to St Paul's – not as blindingly brilliant an achievement as it might seem at first glance, since I believe they had as many to give away as the Loaves and Fishes.

Our brother Brian attended all the same schools, but being three years younger and not a twin did not figure much in our adventures. Naturally he suffered a certain amount of ostracism and bullying, not only as a result of his junior status in the family but also because from birth he was nanny's pet. This post was mostly filled by the redoubtable Nurse Murphy, a long-suffering yet genial Irish woman whose partiality for her youngest charge cost him many a drubbing. So indeed did his quite astonishing mental agility. The humiliation of having your prep done for you by someone three years your junior scarcely makes for an even temper.

The three of us attended St Paul's School at its evacuated locale in the mansion of the Marquis of Downshire at Berkhamsted. An Irish peer of endearing eccentricity, he liked to spend his days playing engine driver on a model railway in the grounds. We, the schoolboys, were co-opted from time to time to fill the roles of firemen, guards and signalmen, and a good time was naturally had by all, until the complications of the railway schedule clashed with our educational timetable and a stop was speedily put to it by the High Master, Mr Walter Oakeshott.

He was a scholar of some apparent vagueness, although he was an expert on the topic of medieval glass. His book on the glass of Winchester Cathedral is still, I believe, the prime authoritative text on the topic. Other subjects he expounded with enormous learning but sometimes, alas, with misleading hype. On one occasion he persuaded the History VIII, of which I was a member, to give up a half-holiday to listen to a talk on what he had described as 'the most important and necessary knowledge you could possess'. Naturally we all thought the lecture was going to be about the birds and the bees, and so willingly traded in our holiday. In the event he lectured us at considerable length and with concomitant aridity on the history of the Javan rudder. Fascinating, but not exactly what we had in mind.

To my regret they had given up the teaching of Greek virtually the term I joined, but there were other compensations, notably the alarming and Olympian figure of one of the ushers (as masters were called), Eynon Smith.

A burly man, attired in cable-stitch blue naval sweater, leather jerkin and broad leather belt instead of the more traditional gown and mortarboard, he would enter the classroom with hoarse cries of 'Read all abaht it', carrying under his arm copies of the morning's newspapers, which he would fling at us. He would then commence his own brilliantly associative way of teaching by shouting, for example, 'Now then, you idle bastards, there are five logical non-sequiturs on the front page of the *Telegraph* this morning. Find them – you've got five minutes.'

With much verbal abuse he would then proceed to make us debate the topics of the day as recorded in the newspapers, as we did so identifying the political bias and criticizing the style. As a finale he would invite us to write an account, for example, of the previous night's football match in the style of Homer or Pliny or Dickens or Damon Runyan or Racine, or in the form of a Shakespearean sonnet.

Smith came at you from all angles – caustic, abusive, searching and exhortatory. Every day was like going fifteen rounds with Marciano, but they were rounds with a man who took the view that between the years of sixteen and eighteen the human mind was at its most fully expanded. No wonder that after two years of this treatment 90 per cent of the History VIII had gained scholarships to either Oxford or Cambridge. (I was the 10 per cent who didn't, somehow managing to fail the Latin exam that entitled me to sit for one in the first place, although on the strength of my papers they gave me a place anyway.) Eynon Smith was alas killed by a doodlebug that unfortunately scored a direct hit on his London home.

He has been greatly missed over the years as a mentor by many members of his form with whom I have discussed the matter, notably Richard Maine (*Observer* film critic and Common Market pundit), James Mossman (of *Panorama* fame) and Jerry Weinstein (a senior executive with the European Atomic Energy Commission), both of whom died young, Dennis Zaphiro (a somewhat sinister soldier of fortune who disappeared from our ken), Edward Behr (editor of *European Newsweek*), Louis Duchêne (right-hand man to European Community architect Monet) and, of course, Peter (playwright). But he had given us enough to travel with.

Between '42 and '44 the war gradually turned in our favour, with Hitler being beaten back from Russia and North Africa, but it was by no means over and conscription still loomed. To this end certain military training seemed a good idea and this instituted a curious if not to say comic set of circumstances.

Monday was OTC Day. As members of the Officers' Training Corps we paraded in uniforms of the same cut and weight, i.e. twenty-four-ounce wool buttoned to the neck, brass buttons, blancoed belt and puttees as British troops had died of suffocation wearing such uniforms before the walls of Pondicherry in southern India over 200 years previously.) My bête noire was a certain Captain H, a Latin master who would always find me the most unpleasant or arduous tasks to perform, usually involving latrines or bushy-topped trees on far horizons that had to be run to.

However, circumstances changed dramatically on Wednesday, which was Home Guard Day. Captain H became Private H and I was his section leader, thus having the command of him. Even more unpleasant and arduous tasks were found for him to perform until a truce was finally called on the occasion of a night exercise on the East Berkshire golf links, in the course of which we took him prisoner. What he was doing on the 'other side' must remain a mystery, but we left him tied to a tree in a rainstorm until he temporized. From then on, Monday and Wednesday afternoons were spent much more comfortably.

But war games were coming to an end, and the real thing was beckoning. In a then more feudal society, the public schools were regularly approached by the heads of the services to recruit likely students for special jobs. A dubious privilege it turned out to be.

After an inconclusive interview with Mr Oakeshott to establish my choice of service, he sent me to see a certain Colonel X in the intelligence service in a building near Victoria Station. The good colonel gave me a piece of French to translate – a bill of lading from the Marseilles railway system that I made a complete hash of. I complained that it was an unfair test as it contained all sorts of highly technical terms that I could hardly be expected to know.

'Sodding schoolboy,' he snarled, 'what do you mean, unfair? Perhaps you would like to tell that to the Gestapo in a few weeks' time when they inevitably pick you up in France? They will probably pat you on the back for trying!' He went on to explain that though he personally didn't give a fig about me, he had men in place in France whom I would inevitably betray by my linguistic incompetence once he had parachuted me in amongst them.

I was naturally crushed by this. I'd had visions of myself in the Scarlet Pimpernel role (James Bond not having been invented at this time). I clearly perceived that the possession of schoolboy French had almost certainly saved my life – for a time anyway – but somehow it was not much consolation. Trench-coats, turned-up collars and soft-brimmed hats; safe houses, code books and rice paper messages (to be swallowed); radio sets concealed behind uniform editions of the classics and revolving bookshelves masking hidden tunnels; screened torches blinking in impenetrable woodlands and men with assorted eyepatches and missing digits – these were the desiderata of the world in which one would die – or at least live – glamorously. Little did I know what was in store for me, however. The colonel, seeing my depressed state as I trudged towards the door, said kindly, 'Never mind, I expect we will manage to find something for you. We will be in touch.'

What resulted was three years of unrelieved hell in the mines as a Bevin Boy. This succinctly unglamorous title was occasioned by the fact that the government in its infinite wisdom had managed to send most of the coal miners off to the war with the result that there was a huge deficiency in the numbers of men actually digging the stuff that eventually allowed the production of the steel for the shells, bombs, anti-aircraft guns, ships, etc., etc. And so we were conscripted, taking our name from the Minister of Labour, Ernest Bevin, and it was off to Castleford for six weeks for Peter and me to be trained as colliers. It was, I believe, the practice of the time to send conscripted twins to the same place. We were later posted to Chislet in the Kent coal fields, a group of mines largely underwater and staffed mostly by resentful Welshmen – resentful of their profession ('I'd never send a boy of mine down the mines,' they'd often say), and resentful of Winston Churchill, who as Chancellor of the Exchequer many years before had treated strikers and men on the dole tremendously harshly. The means test was particularly hated; a jar of jam on the table was a luxury that could cost the owner the dole if detected!

They didn't, curiously enough, resent us as they might have, seeing that from their point of view we were toffs temporarily forced to share their misery. On the contrary they were helpful and sympathetic, teaching us the ropes and being free with helpful tips on the day's work – how to put a tub of coal back on the rails without giving yourself a hernia, for example, or the best way to 'locker up a tub' (stop it by inserting a wooden stick in its wheels without cutting your fingers off), or shore up the roof with timber, or to keep carbide powder off the sandwiches in your snap-tin.

We used carbide lamps underground, which meant a naked flame. Despite this, for some inexplicable reason we weren't allowed to smoke. Shifts were eight hours long, very often waist-deep in water as you were obliged to kneel to hack at the coal. The heat was about 150 degrees Fahrenheit and the atmosphere was poisonous and opaque with coal dust.

Peter was not much luckier. Though he worked on the surface because of an ulcer he had developed, he often had to labour on the tipplers, an antediluvian contraption that up-ended tubs of coal, covering the operator in thick clouds of dust. Workers below and above the surface finished the shift being able to sing 'Mammy'. Luckily we didn't have to use the baths in the living rooms of our digs à la D. H. Lawrence, but bathed in the modern bathhouse with hot and cold running water that was attached to the colliery near the pithead.

Even so, we could never get completely clean. For months after we were demobilized, our skin was pitted with coal dust. Peter, because of his illness, left after two years and went up to Cambridge. I lingered on to complete three and a half. Lord knows why. The war had been over for at least two years by then, but the government wouldn't release me. You can imagine that it was one of the happiest days of my life when I trudged out of the pit for the very last time in February 1948.

One very obvious question must occur to the thinking reader – why did this miner's job come through a colonel of intelligence? I am afraid that it must remain unanswered.

So what did you expect?!

2. Cambridge

After the mines I had to wait nine months before taking up my place at Cambridge, so I joined my father's property business in the minor capacity of rent collector. I felt I owed it to him since I knew he hoped I would eventually come into the firm. Unfortunately the position was too minor for me to get any real idea of what the property business was about. The qualities you required as a rent collector were pertinacity and guile, since about 90 per cent of the tenants you were dunning hadn't the least intention of paying up. Instead they spent the entire time that you were in their street either hiding on the living room floor or under the kitchen table or otherwise babbling exculpatory sob stories through their letterboxes, lachrymose enough to break the heart of a stone golem.

You learned the rules fast. Never arrive at the same time. Elemental disguise was de rigueur – milkman, lending library employee, jobbing gardener, encyclopaedia vendor, water-board official, even onion-seller: all played their part in hoodwinking the reluctant tenants. For many months, in far-flung spots such as Plaistow and Ponders End, I plied the Morton's Fork of the rent collector in innumerable masquerades with varying success. In many cases the householder's evasive tactics won the day and the sad little matter would end in the county court, but we did establish a certain rapport of grudging respect, much like that which I suspect exists between huntsman and fox.

Actually my father never seemed to care if I came back short-changed. Somehow he seemed to expect it, even deriving a certain fatalistic amusement out of it. He had a lot of instinctual sympathy for the poor, or 'skint' as he called them, and he also, a little later, had a horror of being painted with the brush of Rachman (the poisonous landlord who rid himself of inconvenient tenants by having them oppressed). For example, after hearing his cacophonous, ferrous approach to his Chelsea flat as he careened off every third car on the Embankment, I once asked him why he didn't get himself a Rolls-Royce and a chauffeur.

'A Rolls-Royce?' he said in horror. 'Rachman drives one of them! That would never do.'

Similarly, he could never contemplate with equanimity the thought or the sight of people sleeping rough in the streets, and would often house them in empty apartments. On many occasions his reward was to have the accommodated hoboes claiming the protection of squatters' rights and the inequitable Rent Acts.

A balanced, humorous, realistic north-county philosophy kept him saner than his dotty brother Percy. Once, when he stood to win a fortune of £10,000 (in the mid-1930s!) at Aintree on the Grand National, his horse, well clear of the field with only a few yards to go, broke a rein and ran wide of the winning post. About nine years old at the time, I turned to him to express my sorrow at his losing all that money in the last stride. He looked at me solemnly in the manner of someone wishing to impart a truth.

'I didn't lose it, Tony. I never had it in the first place.'

He then laughed and cried out, 'Champagne all round at the bar. That horse gave me a reet good ride this afternoon!'

He was to the end a cheerful realist. He was also in many ways a true Edwardian – dapper, sportif, and in matters sexual both roguishly moustache-twirling and deeply diffident.

So when the time inevitably came that my mother suggested that it was appropriate for him to tell his twin sons the facts of life, we were about thirteen (an interest in the female domestic staff had started manifesting itself), and this shameful prudishness surfaced in a truly hilarious and revealing way.

We were summoned to his study (the billiard room in our Hampstead home) where he sat uncomfortably behind his desk, on which stood prominently his mid-morning half-bottle of Bollinger champagne. He eschewed any cosmetic evasions about the birds and the bees, but plunged straight in with 'Your mother has told me it's about time you boys knew the facts of life. Reet then, here goes.'

Pointing to the bottle he went on, 'Always drink Bollinger! It's sound all through the range from the cheapest to the most pricey. In life you'll find that sometimes you have dough in your pocket, and at other times you are a bit short of the readies, so if you stick to Bollinger you will be able to afford it at any time, and you won't get into any trouble, as you most certainly will if you drink a lot of the other Chinese stuff that's around!' (Chinese was his word for anything strange, unfamiliar, foreign, or dubious.)

As at this date nothing stronger than Tizer (a fizzy apple drink) had passed our lips, this speech naturally fell on stony ground. So we contented ourselves with sagacious nods, but eventually, feeling something more was required, asked if we could sample some of this miraculous standby.

'I don't see why not,' my father said amiably and poured out a couple of glasses. The taste, though at first fairly unpleasant, gradually became more palatable and we asked if we might try some of the forbidden marques in order more clearly to grasp his point. The cook duly brought more half-bottles of other champagnes from the cellar and a good time was naturally had by all.

At last we reeled out of the room, to be confronted by our mother, who had been hovering about outside in the passage anxious to ascertain if the paternal words of wisdom had been assimilated.

As the answer to her first question was a hiccup, she immediately realized we were both legless, and set off furiously for the study.

'Jack,' she screeched at him, 'what have you been doing with the boys?'

'I've been telling them the facts of life, like you asked,' he replied insouciantly. 'They won't get into any trouble now!'

The final echo of this meeting sounded on his deathbed in the Lister Hospital nearly sixty years later. My mother was already in the same hospital with pneumonia, and he had followed her there as a result of a fall in their flat, which broke his leg. Now, lying in bed with one hip replacement of uncertain value and the other leg irreparable, he started to hallucinate, staring at the television high up in the opposite wall in terror believing that someone was trying to climb through the window into the room.

I was standing at the edge of his bed speculating gloomily

what I was going to do with him. Not wishing to put him in a home, I found myself rather wishing he would go, and though I tried to dissimulate it was useless. He read my mind.

'Don't worry, Tony,' he said, for once calling me by my right name, 'I'll be going along presently.' And then added, pointing to a bottle of Bollinger which somewhat surprisingly stood in an ice bucket in the corner, 'Why not have a drink?'

I poured out two glasses and rather foolishly, as tubes protruded from his nose and mouth obviously preventing imbibing, brought him one over. 'I'm sorry I can't do it for you, Tony,' he said mournfully. 'Never mind, sup it oop!'

'But, Pa,' I said, trying to jolly him along, 'you always said never to drink alone.' He looked deep and long into my eyes.

'You won't be alone,' were his last words — a magnificent, dignified, prophetic, paternal blessing.

As I left him I reflected that the dilemma of the Jew after the diaspora is the necessity of being accepted while not being entirely assimilated. This is an almost impossible task because he is never seen clearly — as Bruno Bettelheim writes in *The Informed Heart*, 'the Anti-Semite is not afraid of the comparatively insignificant Jewish individual but of his stereotype of *the Jew*, who is invested with all that is Evil within himself. How dangerous his undesirable inner drives are, and how powerful, he knows only too well. An enumeration of the qualities, which the SS for instance imputed to *the Jew*, is some index of the qualities they tried to deny in themselves. Instead of fighting these qualities in themselves, they fought them by persecuting the Jews.'

I have taken the time to pen this short philosophical disquisition in order to introduce a small but morally perplexing story concerning my father, who was for many years a member of the Westgate-on-Sea Golf Club, and, I believe, the only Jewish one, and also a scratch golfer.

Annually a competition was staged between those who commuted to London and those who did not. This was called the Train Match, and my father dearly wanted to win it. One year he did actually get into the final, but refused to play it because it was scheduled for a Saturday – a holy day on which he didn't play golf. The Committee ardently attempted to persuade him to do so, but he remained adamant. Perhaps this was not as formidable a decision as being asked to recant in medieval times but it nonetheless appeared at the time to be a considerable act of faith even if not of Galileo-like proportions.

That these acts became less obdurate in the succeeding generation is illustrated by the fact that when in 1949 my cousin Robin Spiro was selected to play for Harrow in the annual Eton and Harrow match to be played at Lord's over three days including a Saturday, the news was announced with pride from the pulpit in his synagogue. Even his highly orthodox grandfather offered him a pound for every run he scored, though naturally disapproving. In fact, he made £24, a decent sum in those days, and which while not making him a millionaire, at least assured him he was less constricted than his forebears.

Robin, a founder of the Spiro Institute for Jewish Studies, calls this 'the sandwich generation', meaning it was interleaved between two generations devoted to more vigorous and religious observance. The push towards greater laxity with its concomitant possibilities of greater assimilation was, he believed, generalled by the mothers of the tribe.

I must add that I myself am a member of this 'sandwich

generation' and perhaps the ties had been loosened too much to command my devoted attention.

In October 1948 it was, at last, time for me to take up my place at Cambridge, a university regrettable, as opposed to Oxford, only for its junior age by a few miserable years, its sadly mistaken choice of countryside and its emblematic, thin, washed-out colour blue.

After the murderous, stultifying claustrophobia of the coal mines, Cambridge was paradise. Instead of the daily grind in one of the lower circles of hell, here was a place of soaring medieval buildings to walk amongst and punt amongst, deferential college servants to cosset you, wondrous dining rooms to eat in, activities both sporting and intellectual to indulge in, and lectures to attend or to avoid delivered by the most formidably prestigious minds in the world. Needless to say I went to more of those lectures than the ones I was supposed to be attending for the law course I was doing, mainly I recall to oblige my mother, who for some strange archaic reason – an early crush on F. E. Smith or Lord Curzon I suspect – wanted me to become a barrister. After all, who wouldn't rather listen to a lecture on philosophy by Bertrand Russell or Isaiah Berlin than a grindingly tedious address on the laws of torts or real property by the journeyman university professor of the day?

During my first year in Trinity I roomed with a hearty farmer's son of great geniality and absolutely no aesthetic or intellectual potential whatsoever called Grahame Nesbitt. As I remember, he took the least taxing of the Tripos subjects, geography (sample questions: What is a peninsula? What is the highest mountain in the world? What is a tree-line? etc., etc.).

Eventually he passed it creditably. His friends on the whole were check-shirted hearties who reverenced the aspirations of Erasmus by ripping otters out of their riverbank homes and throwing them to beagles. I'm afraid we didn't have a lot in common, but he covered doggedly enough for me when it came to illicit weekends in London with the entrancing Fanny Bell from the Players Club or Late Joys under Charing Cross Bridge, and whose own late joys in her Sloane Square apartment beckoned more commandingly than the mud and sweat of the sports events at Fenners.

I had met Fanny after the sudden and appalling death of my first love, 'Billie' Williams, a Welsh actress who lived in a basement flat in Victoria Road in Kensington with some harum-scarum thespians of limited means but unquenchable blitheness of spirit. I had learned of her tragic demise in the most unbelievably sensational way possible as a result of a set of circumstances not remotely credible in the most lurid of screen romances.

It was my custom to spend most weekends at my parents' house at Birchington-on-Sea on the Kent coast, a lengthy bungalow on a cliff with a garden terminating in a studio cut into the cliff that was once inhabited by the pre-Raphaelite painter Solomon J. Solomon. On returning to London on Monday morning, I would phone my girlfriend on arrival at Cannon Street Station. This particular day I had changed a half-crown to make the twopenny call by buying the *Evening Standard*. The first edition of the *Standard* was mainly devoted to racing, and any small news items of a sensational nature received unnatural prominence. Receiving no immediate answer and apostrophizing the girl for tardiness as I listened to the endlessly repeated burr-burrs, I eventually opened the folded paper. The front-page headline read: 'Actress Found Dead in Kensington Flat. Electrocuted in Bath!'

Surely it couldn't be my Billie! I read on, hoping against hope. After all, there were twelve million people in London. How unlikely it would be. However, alas, it transpired that the feckless thespians had used a live electric flex as the clothes line above the bath and the insulation had worn thin. With her feet in water, poor Billie had stood up to wash her hair; the back of the hand had touched the exposed wire, and that had been it.

Still stupefied, I made my way to my father's office, where he wisely told me not to get involved – whatever that meant – but of course I involved myself immediately in sending a huge bunch of flowers to the graveyard at Gunnersbury. I remember it cost me about half of what I had in my bank account, a deeply pleasing sacrifice. I also visited the Kensington morgue to view Billie's dead body. It was a sickening mistake. My first love was my first corpse, a waxy glacial effigy of the living, warm woman who'd breathed such life into me. My father in his usual wisdom had been right. 'Don't get involved.'

In some obscure way I think I later came to believe that this incident (coupled perhaps with some unmentionable events in the coal mines) may have led me to accept the 'least likely' theory of Agatha Christie as well as Conan Doyle's famous dictum: 'When you have discarded the impossible, what remains, however improbable it may seem, must be the truth.'

It also may have armoured me against sudden and unlikely death, but I don't think so – not deeply enough. I've somehow been able to avoid the known conclusion that we are all walking on eggshells. I'm mostly deaf to 'time's wingèd chariot hurrying near'. If it hurries, it hurries for others. But also I did come to know that for the first time I was alone, as of course are we all.

No one else really cared about that loss. Propriety won.

Bereft at the graveside, I caught Fanny Bell on the rebound. She had also been Billie's friend. I should add that today she is a highly acclaimed authoress, writing cosy accounts of English village life under the name of Fanny Frewen, suggesting scarcely a hint of her previous raciness but presenting marvellously adroit insights into English country and suburban living.

But back to Cambridge. The first year flew by, with my salient achievement being the assistant editorship of *Granta*, the university humour magazine. Its editor was Arthur Davidson, a wryly amusing Lancastrian lawyer. Together we parodied *London Opinion* (it was the custom to do a parody of another magazine once a year – the previous editor Jonathan Routh had done *Death*, a parody of *Life*, magnificently well).

A little later, it was observed sourly by the university newspaper *Varsity* that *Granta* had no true identity per se but kept on popping up in different eccentric masks and guises. Once it was even distributed in a bottle – a somewhat crazed idea of my younger brother Brian!

But it was always full of life and its irreverent humour was in many instances the clear forerunner of *Monty Python* and *Private Eye*.

'Never take *Granta* for Granted' claim its new owners in their advertising, quoting the *Daily Telegraph*, and of course it has now changed its format and flavour dramatically to become 'The Magazine for New Writing'. With over 70,000 subscribers worldwide, it has obviously completely shed its old parochial and flippant undergraduate trappings and, under its editor Ian Jack and his deputy Liz Jobey, solicits from contemporary writers a range of highly serious contributions in the realms of fiction, memoir, reportage and photography.

We naturally lived in less responsible, larkier climes, and did not confine ourselves to the restraints of only publishing a magazine. We also gave the *Granta* Ball, a chaotic riot that nearly wrecked the Dorothy Café, where it was held and that also nearly had us both sent down. The entrance tickets were the metal tags that prisoners hold up in front of themselves to be photographed, found on a rubbish dump somewhere by Brian, who himself attended the ball dressed alarmingly convincingly as Harpo Marx and who demonically oversaw the entrance proceedings down a long, darkened covered passageway, booby-trapped with flour, soot and treacle. Hair and ballgowns irrevocably ruined, the bewildered and underpleased guests now found themselves confronted by Olsen and Johnson and the entire Hellzapoppin gang, with the former almost immediately devising a fiendishly simple manoeuvre to cause maximum chaos.

'D'ya wanna see a little mayhem?' he asked me. 'Because if ya do, I'm your man.'

As that's precisely what he'd been invited for, and upon my ready assent, he mounted the bandstand and called out to the crowded dancefloor, 'All the gentlemen, put their jackets on their partners.'

Evening jackets were instantly exchanged. I failed to detect much mayhem in the device until he suddenly ordered, 'Now, change partners!'

He repeated this twice more. In the gloom 500 identical hired evening jackets were now inextricably confused and lost, along with their contents of cash and keys. At this point a huge net fell from the ceiling, encompassing the entire company of wildly searching dancers. We the organizers were more satisfied than the male guests! Fisticuffs took place and developed into a riot, completely drowning out the hapless Jessie Matthews, over whose shoulder the cares of the moment resolutely refused to go – she was singing 'Over My Shoulder Goes One Care' – and reducing the Dorothy Café to a windowless ruin.

The *Granta* Ball was banned for the next year, but not the magazine, and I duly became its editor. A number of successful issues culminated in my turn to do a parody. I chose Edward Hulton's *The Leader*, a bright mixture of pictures, articles and profiles, inevitably calling it *The Follower*. Among the contributors were my own brothers Peter and Brian, Leo de Rothschild, Robin McEwen and Richard Mayne, and the cover featured the Gadarene swine by Anthony Pugh. I sent it to London to Stephen Potter, the inventor of Gamesmanship, who was then – in 1950 – the editor of *The Leader* and he was so tickled that he offered me a job on the magazine. From Cambridge to Fleet Street in one jump! Naturally, I was delighted.

Alas it didn't last long – less than a year. At that time television dished most of the picture magazines, including *The Leader*, as well as *Life* (since restored to us) and *Picture Post*, and I was forced to practise at the Bar, whose examination I had somewhat shakily passed.

So what did you expect?!

3. The Bar

Mainly through the offices of a relative, a QC called Leonard Pearl, later Mayor of Marylebone, I found myself in the mostly divorce chambers of a South African barrister called Stansislaus Seifert in the Middle Temple. Also in chambers were the redoubtable Granville Sharpe QC, subsequently Chief Justice of the High Court of Ghana, and Macgilvary Asher, a Scot whose whimsicality was perhaps not best exemplified by his being one of the defending counsel in the Moors Murders case. I once clandestinely listened to the notorious Lesley Ann Downey tape alone in chambers and to this day rather wish I hadn't.

Divorce rather than crime was the speciality of the house, however. It thereby occasioned if not exactly my finest hour then at least my most spectacular, when, in one morning, I contrived an achievement unique in the entire history of the English judicial system. In the space of just two hours I managed to lose two *undefended* divorce cases. This, I can tell you, takes real talent.

It was the normal practice in chambers, I should explain, for the junior to help settle the divorce petition, even drafting it. Thus he would be familiar with not only the causes of action but with the petitioner. On this particular occasion, however, things weren't to be quite so simple. I knew neither the causes

nor the concerned parties in the two petitions thrown at me at
the last minute by my master in chambers, who had suddenly
received far more lucrative papers than the five pounds (plus
two pounds for the clerk) with which mine were marked.

I should also point out that at that time there was a back-
log of cases to be heard and the judges encouraged maximum
speed in dispatching the cases before them. In theory, pleading an undefended divorce should have been like shelling
peas − a series of automatic moves and responses − but in
practice the petitioners on this occasion were embarrassed at
having to appear in a public court in a divorce action, even
though they had been assured by their solicitors that all they
had to do was agree with the questions put by counsel. Unlike
defended cases, in undefended cases you were allowed to 'lead'
− that is to say, suggest the answer − since there was no
dispute. For example, instead of asking, 'What is your name?'
your question would be, 'Your name is Mrs Smith, isn't it?'
I'm sure you might well see that this could be a recipe for
disaster.

On the morning in question I had two cases separated, as it
turned out, by the length of the morning. The first case was a
Mrs E. V. Robertson, who had been married in the parish
church of Berkhamsted on 4 June 1943 (not her real church,
name, nor marriage date).

A frail, frightened, elderly lady stepped into the box. She was
so discombobulated at the sight of the public gallery and the
shame of divorce that she would have answered affirmatively to
the suggestion that her name was Rumpelstiltskin.

In a case of cruelty such as this, you tried to take the least
offensive of the incidents complained of in order to spare the

petitioner's blushes. After all, the judge had the petition in front of him and could read the other offences for himself.

I therefore led, 'Your name is Mrs E. V. Robertson, is it not?'

To this her hopeless cockney voice answered me, 'Oh, yus!'

'And you were married in the parish church of Berkhamsted on the 4th of June 1943?'

'Oh, yus!'

'Now, let's get to the cause of action, Mrs Robertson – cruelty! You were doing your pools one Saturday night in your sitting-room and your husband came home, and, because his dinner wasn't ready, he struck you on the head with a rolling pin. Is that right?'

'Oh, yus.'

'Causing you great distress?'

'Oh, yus, it were 'eavy, the rolling pin. Very nasty. I 'ad an 'orrible 'eadache.'

Resisting the temptation to tell her, as F. E. Smith might have done, that she should have taken two aspirates, I contented myself with a show of sympathy and a brief speech, bringing the judge's attention to the other less savoury incidents of marital warfare mentioned in the petition.

'Yes, yes,' he said testily. 'It's all perfectly clear. You needn't take up any more of the court's time, Mr Shaffer. Decree nisi!'

The rest of the morning passed routinely enough, with other barristers strutting their stuff and the judge feigning weariness interspersed with a complete ignorance of common street knowledge that the average citizen took for granted and occasionally urging speed. Just before lunch, disaster struck. On the bench, half-moon glasses were pushed to the end of the judicial nose.

'I think we've just got time before lunch for one more from you, Mr Shaffer.'

I jumped to my feet to confront a rather more determined lady petitioner than the previous applicant.

'Your name is Mrs B. V. Robertson?' I asked.

'No,' came the firm reply, 'that's an "E" not a "B".'

'So sorry,' I said, blithely failing to detect the huge pit that was beginning to yawn at my feet. 'It must be a typing error. And you were married in the parish church of Berkhamsted on the 5th of June 1943?'

'No,' she riposted stoutly. 'It were the 4th of June.' Memories of a previous 4th of June marriage in the Berkhamsted church stirred uneasily.

'Must be another typing error,' I said unhappily.

'Let's hope that's the last one,' growled the judge. 'I should look to your typing pool, if I were you.'

Hurriedly I proceeded to the first cause of complaint from the petitioner.

'Now, let's see, your husband came home drunk and kicked you up the backside?'

'No, he never did nothink like that.'

The judge threw down his pencil in disgust. 'This is the third time in three questions that your witness has contradicted you,' he barked. 'Can you explain it?'

'My lord,' I said, 'I think I have no recourse other than to treat this lady as a hostile witness' (meaning I should cross-examine her rather than lead her).

'Then pray do so,' he sighed. 'And be quick about it. Anything to make sense of this.'

Turning to Mrs Robertson, I asked her point blank. 'Why exactly are you here, madam?'

''Cos I want a divorce, dun I?'

'Good. At last we agree on something. Then if your husband didn't kick you, what did he do which entitles you to a divorce?'

'Well, I was doing me pools and 'e came in and 'it me on the 'ead with a rolling pin.'

Hell froze over! Stalactites depended from the ceiling. Surely one had heard that story earlier that morning . . . In the instant the matter became clear. It was a trillion to one impossibility. Two women with virtually the same name, give or take a misheard initial, both married in the same parish church, again on a misheard day apart, sue for divorce on the same morning. The papers in the wrong order, an easily made mistake with virtually identical names, a panicky witness who would agree with anything, and Bob's your uncle.

The judge froze in his seat and icily requested my presence in his chambers.

'Mr Shaffer,' he boomed as I entered, 'have you any idea of what you have achieved in my court this morning!?'

'I'm beginning to have a pretty good notion, my lord,' I quailed.

'Then let me make it absolutely crystal clear,' he fumed. 'As far as I know you are the only person in the history of the English judiciary ever to lose two undefended divorce cases in one morning. I suppose I should really congratulate you.'

Useless to point out that I had never seen either petitioner, and that the first one had agreed with my every question, and that furthermore the bench had continually urged speed.

'Besides, in her case,' I said, 'you yourself gave a decree nisi to her.'

He gave me a withering look. 'On perjured evidence,' he snapped. 'And I can hardly grant a decree to the woman currently in the box on the same set of facts! Thus two women, perfectly entitled to divorces, cannot be given them. And furthermore, it's all on Legal Aid!'

After a long gloomy pause for reflection, he added charitably, 'You'd better have a sherry – a very large one!'

Not all my cases were so disastrous. I once had a splendid Perry Mason-type victory where a single falsehood irretrievably damned the witness as a liar and an unsuspected criminal. The case involved a long-distance lorry driver driving up the dual carriageway from Southampton docks on a foggy night. A man had unfortunately driven into the back of the lorry and was instantly killed. The lorry driver's evidence, established in cross-examination, showed that he was a professional of many years' standing, and it also revealed that, because he knew his back lights were out and he still had the use of his front beams, he was proceeding cautiously at no more than twenty-five to thirty miles an hour. I somehow intuited that the man was lying but (stupidly) could not shake his story of prudence and caution. Fortunately the court rose early, leaving me the night to reflect on the matter.

I finally decided to experiment in my own car and having removed the back lights I drove round the unfrequented Edwardes Square at the rear of my Earls Terrace flat. After 100 yards, with many a nervous glance over my shoulder, I understood immediately why he was lying. I drove home as swiftly as possible and called the police to examine the contents of his lorry.

Next morning, when hostilities were resumed in a style Perry Mason's assistant Della Smith would have approved of, I went straight for the jugular.

'Now then, you knew your back lights were out and that your front lights were working.'

'Yes, I told you so. That's why I was going along with maximum caution, twenty-five miles an hour max.'

'If the only place danger could have come from was your lightless rear, why were you going slowly?' I asked triumphantly. 'Surely the prudent thing for an experienced professional lorry driver like you to have done was to have driven as quickly as possible to a turn-off or lay-by in order to remove the danger in the shortest possible time?'

There was no answer.

'The only reason,' I continued, 'is that you're lying – aren't you? You didn't know your back lights were out. You were driving extra slowly not to attract the attention of the police. Isn't that the case?'

'Nah. Why the 'ell should it be?' was the panicked response.

'Because of what was inside your lorry,' I concluded smugly. 'And on this point I should like to call Police Sergeant X to give elucidatory evidence.'

The police sergeant duly described the contents of the lorry – a load of television sets and other domestic electrical equipment filched from Southampton docks. The result was a five-year sentence for the lorry driver and satisfactory compensation for the estate of the dead motorist, since it had been proved that the luckless lorry driver had been driving dangerously.

Notwithstanding this trial, and the fact that my master in chambers had given me the 'one day all this will be yours' type speech, I felt the need to move on.

So what did you expect?!

4. Marriage – Number 1

After the hapless Billie Williams and Fanny Bell came the wholly original, uniquely talented, deliriously camp and ludicrously voluptuous Fenella Fielding, at that time one of the nation's sex icons. We were semi-engaged for a couple of years and only a certain neurotic self-preoccupation in her frightened me off marriage.

Helping to make my mind up about the inadvisability of marriage was a disastrous weekend visit to my parents' house in Birchington-on-Sea. She insisted on coming to the dinner table in a succession of flame-coloured dresses slashed to the navel and continuously addressed my venerable papa as 'dahling'. Needless to say my mother's reaction was a blast from the Arctic, in which Miss Fielding's overt charms tended to suffer from extreme frostbite.

Perhaps I was over-influenced by parental disapproval but subsequent reflection has convinced me of the improbability of the success of a liaison underpinned by such dotty theatrical loucheness. All the same there have been many times when I have regretted it, and remembered with keen pleasure for example her performances in *Valmouth* and her cabaret act at the Café de Paris where she topped the bill immediately after Noël Coward and before Marlene Dietrich. I wondered why she never got married, and hoped desperately that it had nothing to do with my own defection.

A few months later I did marry a beautiful but simple creature called Henrietta Glaskie, mainly I now believe to oblige my mother, and of course the whole thing was a disaster.

We honeymooned at arm's length in Ibiza and on return to London my father kindly accommodated me in one of his properties, Earls Terrace on the north side of Edwardes Square in Kensington.

My (almost) child-bride seemed perplexed by the sophistications of life and seemed either unable or reluctant to contribute to the dinner-time conversation with our guests. In order to assist her I suggested that she might perhaps stock her mind with the events of the day as reported in some of the less complex tabloids.

With this end in view, I duly purchased for her the *Daily Mirror* over which she puzzled for hours — her pretty face puckered in plainly bewildered thought. Finally I asked her solicitously whether I could help in any way.

The seraphic face lifted and the gorgeous brown eyes locked on mine pleadingly.

'There is just one thing you could explain,' she said apologetically. '*Who* is Europe?'

I knew at that moment the marriage was over. This was not to be my last matrimonial voyage, but nothing in subsequent adventures prepared me for the realization that as La Rochefoucauld puts it, 'No matter whom you marry, you will discover the next morning that you have married someone else.'

So what had *I* expected?!

5. Advertising

After four years of timewarp pomposity – of close friends addressing me by my surname; of young men pretending to be nonagenarians; of waistcoats and half-moon eyeglasses; of red tape and grovelling 'If your ludship pleases' and genteel poverty (remember, a barrister can't advertise) – I decided I'd had enough. To contemplate another forty or so years of it was an impossibility and in addition my hand was forced by the generous speech of my master in chambers. In all fairness, if I didn't want it others most assuredly did, so that night in 1955 I knew I had to come clean. I went to the movies, a much used way of dealing with a problem, where I found myself contemplating the advertisements of Pearl and Dean.

I realized that not only were they better made than the feature but also that a knowledge of their multifarious, dazzling techniques was a certain key to the door of commercial advertising that was coming next year on television. By leaving the Bar, I would be momentarily somewhat behind the pack, but acquiring these skills would put me not only up with it, so to speak, but in front of it when commercial television came in, since I could bet that very few people in the country would have the faintest idea of how to write commercials.

The next morning, after some difficulty, I made myself an

appointment to see Byron Lloyd, the managing director of Pearl and Dean in Dover Street.

'What makes you think you can write these things?' he asked me brusquely. After I had outlined my midget writing accomplishments he added, 'And why do you want to write them?'

I explained, and then he asked me what I was doing at the moment. On hearing that I was a barrister, he asked, surprised, 'Bit of a come-down?'

'More a lateral step,' I responded. 'More of a step into the future than a come-down.'

Eventually I said that I was prepared to work for nothing for a couple of months, after which he could chuck me out or pay me the going rate. He seemed flummoxed by this, so I pursued my advantage.

'I mean to say, who is using that desk there?' pointing to an empty desk in the adjacent room.

'I don't believe anyone is,' he muttered.

'Well, I could start using it from next Monday,' I said. 'And as I say, it won't cost you a penny.'

He threw in his hand. I had made him an offer he couldn't refuse, and also proved a theory of mine – that you can get into any profession, however 'closed shop', if you are prepared to work for nothing. After all, within a couple of months you should be able to know enough of the ropes – in this case the advertising agencies who commissioned work from the firm – to be able to survive on your own.

The techniques of writing and film-making had to be acquired, but P&D was something of a pressure cooker and you learned fast. Very often you were likely to write the ads in the morning and shoot them in the basement studio that afternoon.

On my first afternoon I recall squinting unhappily through the camera, saying, 'I can't get it all in without making it look too small. A passing director and future friend, Peter Duffell, asked me derisively, 'Ever heard of a lens, mate?'

On the whole it was a happy time at P&D. Byron Lloyd obviously decided that he couldn't countenance me working for no pay and offered what in 1955 was the very useful sum of eleven pounds per week, which at the end of the two months he doubled. I would have had to have done only two undefended divorce cases a week to have made the same money, but in that respect I never looked back or gave the Bar a second thought. Instead I was working in some realistic if bastardized form of creativity, and was learning to tell a story in seven, fifteen, thirty, forty-five and sixty seconds, and then even in two minutes. This is a precious skill, instilling in you a sense of 'real' time as well as dramatic time, so that even today I can edit speeches and accompanying action in my head with the accuracy of a stopwatch, which was our mentor and taskmaster. I can still count a minute blindfolded to a single second's accuracy, and hopefully this ability has excised some tedium from my creative work.

Before I leave the subject of commercials I would like to dilate a little on a few of the favourite spots that my partner Robin Hardy and I made later when in 1960, helped by my father, we formed our own production company, Hardy Shaffer and Associates, with offices at Buckingham Gate, near the Palace, and later in Eccleston Street, near Victoria Station.

Once, we had to illustrate the almost three-dimensional quality of the colour reproductions in an art magazine devoted to a different famous painter each week. We actually conceived one of the Goya 'black pictures', in which a little boy has a cat on a string hungrily staring at a bird in a cage, as a real set, moving the camera on a curved track round behind the figures, thus making them three-dimensional. This piece of film was used exiguously – and almost subliminally – intercut with other normally photographed pictures from the magazine so that the viewer only partially glimpsed the effect and really couldn't believe his or her eyes but accepted the claim for three-dimensional reproduction. This became an acclaimed prize-winner at the International Advertising Film Festival in Cannes.

Other prize-winning goodies were some McVitie's biscuit spots for my great friend John Ritchie, whom I'd met at Lytle's, a strange advertising agency run by an American pirate called Charlie Lytle, where I briefly shared the writing chores with a genial ruffian called Rex Berry. Ritchie later became managing director of Collett Dickinson and Pearce and set a policy that produced some of the funniest commercials in the country – Hamlet cigars and Heineken beer spring to mind.

In the McVitie's commercials we would be using half-cartoon, half-real objects, a technique first developed by Saul Steinberg employing for example, most simplistically, a long-case grandfather clock 'wearing' a hat and with slippers placed at its base with added cartoon arms on the wall behind it holding – naturally – a packet of McVitie's biscuits. An empty white suit walking through belching traffic for a dry-cleaning firm was another of my favourites, as was a journey round a pub for Courage's brewery, missing the drinkers but catching, just too late, fragments of their activities – the pint of beer rocking as it has just been put down, the cigarette tossed into the ashtray, the dart being plucked out of the double twenty, or the mushroom skittle teetering on the edge of the hole on the bar billiards table, all set to a sonorously declaimed piece of Dr Johnson about the unrivalled comforts of a 'tavern or inn'.

Perhaps the most sensationally original was a clutch of commercials for the Egg Board directed by Joan Littlewood in Plaistow, in the East End of London, for Shelley Shelton, the creative director of Mather and Crowther, and featuring a gang of tearaway kids, Avis Bunnage and Geoffrey Palmer, more recently a television star in the company of Judi Dench.

I had gained the directorial prowess of the eclectic and somewhat revolutionary Joan in exchange for filming, for free, a rocket take-off for the moon for a panto which she and her husband Gerry Raffles (the nefarious Mr Red Socks – 'Scream, kids, when you see them!') were doing at Wyndham's. Predictably most of these ads were unusable, not at all remotely subscribing to the prescribed commercial lengths, but they won us lots of lovely prizes and did wonders for our showreel.

Another ad is perhaps worth mentioning, for its bizarre details as much as anything else. It was one of a clutch of spots made for Ford Cars for a producer at J. Walter Thompson in New York called Byron McKinney.

The location was a bullring in Cascais, Portugal, a location selected as much for its picturesque charm and peaceable bulls as much as for anything else. In Portugal the bulls aren't killed, but instead, after performing with picadors and matadors, are garlanded with flowers and allowed to leave the ring. This of course produces a vast residue of elderly ring-smart tauruses of considerable wiliness and doubtful amiability, something no doubt we should have borne in mind after having received an objurgation from McKinney to take particular care of the single brand new, bright red – and irreplaceable – car sent over from Detroit for the shoot.

The amusing idea of the commercial was to show off the manoeuvrability of the automobile by showing its owner unknowingly drive into the bullring which lay at the end of a maze of narrow, twisting streets, and there be forced to take evasive action as the beast suddenly charged.

I had of course assured McKinney that we had been at great pains to secure the innocuous services of the most benevolent bull in the country. As it was so decrepit, the only question was whether it would last out the day.

McKinney seemed well satisfied as we stood together high up in the bleachers watching the animal in question amble into the ring, peaceably following a little dog that frisked between its legs. The 'hero' – the car – stood placidly gleaming in the sun, some 100 yards or so away from where the bull had come to rest. All seemed ready for the cameras to start rolling.

'It looks all right,' said Byron affably. 'Big but harmless, eh?'

'As a little mouse,' I assured him.

'Great,' he continued. 'Remember, there's no back-up car!'

'You don't have to remind me,' I assured him. 'Just think Ferdinand!' (A reference to a placid, cowardly cartoon bull who preferred to smell flowers rather than to fight.) 'We'll have this whole thing in the can in two shakes of a lamb's . . .'

My voice trailed off as the bull suddenly lowered its head and tossed the little dog a clear 200 yards over our heads. Ripped entrails splattered our clothes with blood as it flew by.

'It's just a little bit more lively than we thought,' I quavered. 'But it'll settle down.'

'I sure as hell hope so,' said Byron dubiously, brushing chunks of the hound's tripes off his Brooks Brothers blazer.

'There's no question of it,' I assured him. 'He came off the Ark. He can scarcely walk.'

At that moment the red car caught the bull's attention. Again, it lowered its head and charged. It went right through the car, which fell into two neat halves, and kept going.

So what did you expect?!

'Any suggestion what we do now?' asked Mr McKinney laconically.

Actually, I hadn't. In the end we somehow cobbled it all together from a hundred close-ups of the shattered vehicle interspersed with trick shots of the charging bull and the driver's terrified face.

Thus it is obvious that montage is the mother of invention.

I have jumped straight from Pearl and Dean without reference to the intervening years, first at the Film Producers' Guild and then at Television Advertising. The former was a faintly old-fashioned institution in the Strand which had animation studios of great skill and complexity in Maiden Lane and live-action studios in a converted cinema at Barnes. I lived a pretty harum-scarum life in the Dickensian court we occupied behind Finch's wine bar in the Strand, protected from the occasional wrath of the board by an ex-cameraman and antique Bentley aficionado called Ray Elton, who viewed my eccentric, hungover, chronic lateness with tolerant amusement. The Oxley camera was our trump card, presided over by a modest genius called Gillie Potter. There was seemingly nothing technical he could not accomplish, and selling his prowess to advertising agents was easy, as indeed was selling people of the calibre of Nic Roeg and Dick Lester as two of the contracted directors.

Next door to our closeted hideaway was the Civil Service Stores, an institution of even more archaic attributes. Looking one day into the fustian windows, I fell to wondering what on earth it had to entice anyone who was living in the twentieth rather than the nineteenth century through its doors. Wine! was the inspired guess, and thus I came to meet the incredibly subtle yet vengeful Mr Whitehead. He was subtle in two ways. Firstly, he possessed a mental adroitness to rival that of Machiavelli and, secondly, physical suppleness. He had at one time been a member of Charlie Chaplin's troupe the Mumming Birds and now, at the age of eighty-eight, he could still high-kick his hand held straight out from his shoulder. He had, however, rather like Iago, been passed over by his bosses for preferment, as had his entire wine department, and he took his own magnificent revenge. He relabelled expensive bottles of rare burgundy so that, for example, the mighty Richebourg or La Tâche would appear as the humble Hermitage, appropriately priced. His many friends – and he himself (since he was permitted to take home a bottle of wine a day) – drank like princes for many months for infinitesimal sums of money. To this day I often order a bottle of Hermitage in restaurants out of nostalgic affection.

Techniques of acquiring business at the Guild revolved chiefly around screening showreels to ad agency producers in order to demonstrate the prowess of our directors in cartoon, animation and live action. Many commercials were a mélange of all three, involving enormous skill and cost (more was spent per frame on commercials than on feature films). We also entertained clients, which essentially meant filling them up with food and booze. If this sounds like fun I can assure you that on the whole it wasn't. Day after day one would sit in Soho, in grand restaurants such as Kettners and L'Étoile and the White Tower, opposite people in whom one had little interest except the need to extract commissions, watching them stuff themselves with endless unnecessary courses and having to do likewise out of politeness. It ultimately became distasteful. The waistline expanded, as did one's detestation of subservient waiters, tortured table napkins and roaring spirit heaters.

After a couple of years, I moved on to TVA or Television Advertising, a similar outfit with whom I made a ludicrous contract under which I was to receive 10 per cent of the gross of any contracted business I brought in. Quite obviously, the larger the budget, the more I received, and, as I did the budgeting, the temptation to make them of *Ben Hur*-like proportions was almost irresistible. The managing director was Colonel Heald, a former equerry of the Duke of Edinburgh and a most charming man with absolutely no background in either advertising or film-making. In spite of his charm and ex-military old Englishness, neither he nor his board honoured my contract and I ended up working for a couple of years for virtually nothing. Eventually, when the company went into bankruptcy, I received a payment of two shillings in the pound on what I was owed.

During this time I had met Robin Hardy in America. Eventually we formed our own production company, based on a showreel of some remarkably imaginative Alcoa commercials made in the States by Hardy, as well as a handful of my own contacts from the ranks of agency producers and a loan of £10,000 from my father. We also inherited a Mancunian accountant called Tony Heaford, who was run financially ragged by the capricious and often childishly self-willed Hardy, whose traits were to contribute to our eventual dissolution.

While all this had been going on, I had met and married in 1962 a gorgeous francophone model. She had worked for many of the great Parisian couture houses – Yves Saint Laurent and Christian Dior amongst them – and as a result was inclined to be skeletal. As a further result of a domineering, Russian jeweller father whose views of domesticity were closely aligned to those of Peter the Great, she was also inclined to be inaudible. Her name was Carolyn Soley. She was an unerringly tasteful dresser, a formidable linguist, and quite clearly one of the finest cooks in the country.

As if this were not enough, she gave me two little girls of quite unique beauty and mettlesome personality – the cuddle-some Claudia, and the premature, more slightly constructed Cressida. All in all, it was too good to last.

But now the main event was coming up, even though, to be honest, I had always imagined it would, in an arrogant out-of-focus sort of way. Perhaps I should have been warned by Montaigne (*Essays III–IX*) that there is no greater enemy to those who would please than expectation.

6. *Sleuth* – The Main Event

What I have termed the main event – it's certainly the event for which I am best known – was a play that was to run eight and a half years in the West End and four and a half on Broadway. It is only one of two straight plays (the other being *Arsenic and Old Lace*) to do over 2,000 performances in both places and, according to Samuel French, has been produced every day somewhere in the world since it was written back in 1969. I refer of course to *Sleuth*. But enough of vainglorious statistics. Let me try and tell you how it all came about.

Making commercials had become as unfulfilling as pleading cases. My brother Peter, whom I had briefly encountered in New York on my way through to Puerto Rico to do a clutch of Pepsi-Cola commercials, had said to me, 'Every time we meet you're on your way to make some TV spots for some ghastly product or other. Is this really the way you want to live your life? You're a writer – why don't you stop avoiding it and get on with it?'

He knew that together we had written a couple of detective stories under the pen name of Peter Antony, *How Doth the Little Crocodile?* and *Withered Murder*, both published by Gollancz. (Peter had first written another, *The Woman in the Wardrobe*, published by Evans and with drawings by Nicholas Bentley.)

'Lock the door, and tell nobody'– Great-grandfather.

Marked for life (see initials on costumes). Crabbing, Westgate-on-Sea, 1932.

Boulevardiers, circa 1934. The three brothers.

The Scourge of the Spanish Main.

'I like anniversaries, being always minded to drink my cup
of life to the bottom, and take my chance of the sweets and bitters.'
T. H. Huxley. My parents – a milestone wedding anniversary.

'Without a family, man alone in the world, trembles with the cold.'
André Maurois, *The Art of Living*. Us, circa 1942.

On the razzle, with me putting on the ritz, circa 1948.

A few years later!

EYE WITNESS ACCOUNT OF HOW LEVIN FREDMAN IS THOUGHT TO HAVE
LOST HIS LIFE.

. . . .

Shortly after lunch on May 13th,1940, a flight of 615
Squadron (A.A.F.HURRICANES) to-gether with 3 flights from
other squadrons (making a total of 36 aircraft) serving
with B.E.F. were ordered off from Vitry-en-Artois, to
patrol Brussels at 20,000 feet. Our aircraft, in close
formation, were at about 10,000 feet on their way to
Brussels when what appeared to be about 20 ME 109's were
seen about 8 miles away on the starboard beam. Fredman,
who until then had been flying in formation, suddenly
broke away for no apparent reason and flew straight towards
the enemy as though to take them on single handed. The
enemy aircraft changed into battle formation and Fredman
was last seen in their midst. The flight took place too
far away to see exactly what happened but it feared that
Fredman almost certainly lost his life in aerial combat.
He was called up on his wireless but there was no reply.
Our patrol continued.

It is remembered that Fredman gave his gold watch (a present
from his sister) to the Squadron Doctor for safe keeping
about two days before his last flight. The Doctor (F/L.
Stevenson - Cromie) was later killed in a bombing raid.

*There is just a chance that he may have baled out
and been taken prisoner.*

. . . .

My hero!

My first wife, Henri.

My second wedding
reception as I embrace my
mother-in-law on leaving,
with new bride, Carolyn,
in the foreground,
sporting her dashing
'going away' outfit.

'Say cheese!' – *en famille* in the garden of our Somerset schoolhouse.
Claudia, on my knee, is six, and Cressida, on Carolyn's, three.

Claudia and Cressida, now grown up and gorgeous.

Diane in mid-sixties *Spotlight* photograph.

'If you marry, you will regret it; if you do not marry you will also regret it' – Søren Kierkegaard. Marriage number three, in our wedding finery in the garden of Karnark, North Queensland.

The terrible twins again – the author somewhat more posed on this occasion in a photo by Prince Stefano Massimo.

Stepson Jason Connery in costume for *The Train*, a film about Lenin.

This was an odd sort of partnership, with me providing the basic plots and Peter and I penning alternate chapters.

Later, in a sneaky effort to secure some sales, I reviewed *Withered Murder* astonishingly favourably as editor of *The London Mystery* magazine under a sobriquet – Newgate Calendar, I think it might have been. 'The best detective story this century . . . Sensationally adroit – dwarfs Agatha Christie' etc., etc. These words were to appear on the crimson wrapper of the Gollancz publication, to the subsequent chagrin of our editor there when he discovered the matter. Despite this chicanery, sales were comparatively modest, and the books today remain something of a curiosity, though we have *so far* resisted *numerous* offers to republish them.

With Peter's objurgation ringing in my ears and with the help of a clandestinely administered tab of LSD by an American girl, in addition to the fact that our business was most probably about to be bought by a vast Swiss conglomerate, I formed the intention that I had better start writing.

This was easier said than done. I first had to inform my partners Robin Hardy and Denis Abey of my intention. Kindly they sought to dissuade me, as they would to someone sadly deranged, then they tried to provide a safety net, a clause in my severance contract that would allow me to return after a year's sabbatical – plainly a most subversive one. With that I wouldn't have done a thing and then returned after a year, having achieved nothing. With more courage than I felt, I vehemently rejected it. What I needed was terror – the blank page – the absence of an expense account, chauffeured car, regular income and the cheerful, if deceiving, badinage and camaraderie of old hacks and chums.

I also needed the unquestioning support of my wife Carolyn, which I got unstintingly. When I haltingly told her that most of the above goodies were things of the past and that she was going to have me at home all day, she said, 'Thank God! I thought you would never have the guts to do it.'

So there I was in my study in my extraordinary Queen Anne house in the Putney Bridge Road (a lunatic fire-trap interior of linseed-oiled pine), notebooks and sharpened writing instruments at the ready, a wife and two small children to feed, clothe and educate, with no visible means of support, determined against all reasonable odds to become a playwright!

And it was this lack of visible means of support that was eventually to prove the inspiration for me in more ways than one – and I don't only mean financial terror.

After a month or so of busy scribbling, I'd completed the first act. Upon reading it through, I realized that I had written the most threadbare, hackneyed, overused format known to the West End – a marital quartet consisting of husband, wife, mistress and lover. Was this what I had left my business for in such a blaze of courage and saluting trumpets?

Gloomily I contemplated the manuscript, wondering what to do next. Throw it in the fire and return to my company seemed the likeliest answer. A view from the very bottom of the barrel is the perspective of desperation, and it often generates enlightenment. Thus it was that at this moment my eye happened to fall on a coffee-table book of Greek temples. Idly turning the pages, I came to notice that as time passed the Greeks gradually reduced the number of columns on which the roof and architrave rested, and that as a result of having fewer visible means of support the structure appeared mightier and more impressive. The conclusions were easy to draw.

What did I need with the routine sexpot mistress, with her endless double entendres, or the equally routine wife, with her endless nagging and tart put-downs? With infinite relief I removed both of them at one stroke, and also for good measure killed off at the end of the first act the lover, thus leaving myself with only one character with whom to complete the entire second act!

Very fortunately, having thus painted myself into an inescapable corner, as the serial writers in boys' comics used to say when an insoluble dilemma faced their hero, with one bound Jack was free. The answer came almost immediately. Maybe thirty years later there may be some people who still do not know what that answer was, so I shan't reveal it here. Suffice it to say it was greeted with the type of *réclame* boastfully outlined previously.

The play was first sent to the doyen of West End producers, Binky Beaumont, who though flatteringly admirous nonetheless rejected it. 'Everyone will know the trick within a week, dear, no one will keep quiet about that. It won't last a fortnight! Sorry.'

That he was completely wrong, and that they did keep quiet, he handsomely acknowledged a few years later at a splendid dinner by way of apology at his house in Lord North Street. I remember him saying that you can never underestimate the British sense of fair play, which I suppose makes the story of the cabby, the Japanese tourists and *The Mousetrap* all that more poignant. The cabby, untipped after a fifty-pound trip from

Heathrow Airport with a party of Japanese tourists who had asked him to take them to *The Mousetrap*, yelled after them as they entered the theatre, 'The ——— did it!' (giving them the identity of the murderer).

You may now see how I also respect this sense of fair play, particularly with regard to a woman such as Agatha Christie, who had been my seminal mentor.

Jumping ahead of myself by about three years, after we had been playing at the St Martin's for over that length of time without dropping a seat, I was instrumental, to my eternal shame, in having us thrown out of that wonderful theatre by its owner, Peter Saunders. We were replaced by the quite appalling *Mousetrap*. It came about in this way.

Down at Pinewood Studios we were shooting the film of the play with Laurence Olivier and Michael Caine, and I'd suggested to the director Joseph Mankiewicz that it might be a good idea in the shooting scene for a bullet to pass through the silver-framed photograph of Agatha Christie signed, for our fictional detective writing hero Andrew Wyke, 'Yours in admiration, love Agatha'.

Like all Americans, he suggested consulting a lawyer to see if we could get permission. Needing the decision during my lifetime, I merely called Mr Cork at Collins, then Agatha's publishers, and explained the position. Astonishingly he was back to us in under ten minutes, saying that the Dame would be tickled pink but that there would be a price. With a heavy heart, I asked how much, and he said that she had never seen *Sleuth*. So here was one of the richest writers in the world, with something like 400 million copies of her books published worldwide in a trillion languages looking for a couple of freebies. Of course I said that I would be delighted to oblige, but that there would be a further penalty on my part: I had never met her and would like to take her and her husband Max Mallowan to dinner. So all was arranged – there was to be no publicity and the restaurant had to be within a stone's throw of the theatre. The latter stipulation was easily met – the famed theatrical restaurant the Ivy is less than a hop and a jump from the theatre – but the first proved impossible.

The studio of course sent about thirty photographers, for which I was later eternally grateful, otherwise I wouldn't have the accompanying picture. (Look very closely at the scarf!) On seeing them, she immediately moved towards the Ambassadors Theatre, some scant twenty yards to her right, so that *The Mousetrap* would be in the background. Just as quickly, I hauled her poor stick-like limbs back so that *Sleuth* would form part of the background too (you can just see it gleaming in the dark).

Once in the cosy atmosphere of the Ivy, I asked Agatha how she had liked the performance and whether she had spotted the trick. Very charmingly, she said with more than a hint of self-parody, 'I'm supposed to say "Yes". After all, I'm meant to be the "Queen of Crime".'

Referring to a piece of stage chicanery based on disguise, she said, 'I did wonder why you had employed such a terrible actor.'

'You could say the same thing to Billy Wilder about casting Marlene Dietrich in the film of *Witness For the Prosecution*,' I replied tartly, but added swiftly, 'it's of course the best stage thriller of them all. The last ten minutes are incomparable.'

'Except for *Sleuth*,' she replied gallantly, adding the nicest words ever said to me, 'You know, the mantle now falls on you!'

Compliments whizzed back and forth for a couple of moments, which I brought to a summary halt by criticism of *The Mousetrap*.

'It's hardly your best work, Dame Agatha,' I said. ,

'I know,' she agreed. 'It's a silly little piece. I wish it would go away.'

Later that evening, after the Christies had left, shoehorned into a Mini, my brother Peter (who had gatecrashed my date) and I, curious about what notices *The Mousetrap* had originally received and primed by some splendid Armagnac, crossed the road to the Ambassadors to find out. We searched in vain for *The Times*, the *Telegraph*, the *Guardian*, the *Observer* et al. but instead discovered clips such as 'A great evening in the theatre – *Gardener's Gazette*', 'The thriller of the century – *Stamp Collector's Weekly*', etc., etc.

I said I thought I ought to update them. Borrowing a couple of sandwich boards from the adjacent St Martin's, I propped them up against the walls of the Ambassadors and wrote on them, 'A silly little piece – *A. Christie*' and 'I wish it would go away – *Agatha Christie*'.

Well pleased with our evening's work, we tottered off home.

About 8.30 the next morning the phone wasn't ringing so much as dancing on its receiver. My producer Michael White was on the line, and he wasn't friendly.

'What the hell were you up to last night?' he asked nastily.

'Well, I had rather a heavy date,' I began.

'I know all about that,' he interrupted. 'And as a result of your activities we have been thrown out of the St Martin's Theatre!'

I couldn't believe this after three years without dropping a seat, and said so.

'Peter Saunders' – the owner of both the St Martin's and the Ambassadors – 'just called me and said that you were seen last night defacing his theatre with disparaging messages.'

'They were the author's own opinions,' I expostulated.

'Even so,' he went on, 'that's the position. We've been given our marching orders. You've a clause in your contract about moral turpitude and behaving yourself in public, which apparently you have violated by defacing his theatre.

'Then,' I replied, 'you had better take us to a place where we won't be dogged by such a nitpicking prig.'

We moved to the Garrick to run a further five years – a 1,000 seater as opposed to a 680-seater – while Peter Saunders moved *The Mousetrap* from the 480-seater Ambassadors into St Martin's, obviously the object of the whole exercise. Thus financially we were both better off, but with the likely loss of the St Martin's for the rest of our lives the London theatre is equally obviously not.

I suppose I had better tell you a little of just quite how this piece became an astonishing tour de force, which means going back to the early days in the rehearsal room before – as Caryl Brahms and S. J. Simon have it in *The Bullet in the Ballet* – rather than being a tour de force we were 'forced to tour'.

The scene was a bleak, snowbound church hall in Camden Town, significantly lacking in heat. Clifford Williams, after some demur, had agreed to direct, doing so with the assistance of a young man known as Nick the Gum, not for any orthodontic protuberance that might have explained the sobriquet but very simply on account of his invariable footwear – ravaged gum shoes through the copious apertures of which peeped his sodden grey socks. They may have been comfy but they were certainly insufficient for snow-girded Camden Town, as were also the miserable holed gym shoes used as an alternative, occasioning his other nickname of Nick the Gym.

Carl Toms had designed us a magnificent Norman manor house (an architectural invention, since apparently they built only castles and religious structures). There was a ridiculous first attempt which had consisted of a replica of the standard Agatha Christie Cornish cottage set – blue cyclorama, seagulls and an acre of chintz that I myself had stupidly asked for, believing it would provide an ironic comment on the battle between the two principals. But the revamped model had lots of stone, Romanesque pillars, sinister mullions and hideyholes, a huge window bisected by a gallery, and a gorgeous, uneven, flag-stoned floor – in short, the very apotheosis of Gothic follies.

In addition to our actors, Anthony Quayle and Keith Baxter, we had some very minimalist portraits supplied by Philip Farrar, Harold K. Newman and Roger Purnell. We spent the first two weeks at the table, reading and analysing the text and doing absolutely no blocking. I began to think that we might between us all argue and rationalize the whole thing out of existence. For example, we couldn't even agree on a title. I had called it *Anyone for Tennis?*, but Quayle rightly insisted it was too puny and derisory and would lead to us not being taken seriously. So we erected a blackboard and every day either Baxter, Quayle, Williams or I wrote a title on it to see if it would work as a marquee name and be more than just an auditory success.

I recall in particular how Quayle produced a brilliant one – a Shakespearean one, of course, as befitted an ex-director of Stratford's Royal Shakespeare Company, taking it from the last lines of *Hamlet*, spoken by Horatio. Quayle quoted:

> So shall you hear
> Of carnal, bloody, and unnatural acts,
> Of accidental judgements, casual slaughters,
> Of deaths put on by cunning . . .

Slowly he wrote on the blackboard *Deaths Put On By Cunning*.

We all stared at it, mesmerized. There was no question it was right on the nose. But by the end of the day I knew it wasn't right.

'I'm sorry, Tony,' I said, 'but I just can't see the average punter calling up Keith Prowse and asking for "Two stalls for *Deaths Put On By Cunning*." They'll never remember it, let alone be able to pronounce it.'

Grudgingly he agreed. It was my turn.

'What is this play about?' I asked the company. 'Surely it is concerned with the difference between pre-war and post-war Britain, as exemplified by the attitudes of the fictional amateur detectives who were always superior to the blundering professional police. Now, what was that figure called? Surely it was known as a "sleuth"?'

And with that I wrote it up on the blackboard, where it stared back at us, an obviously crisp, intriguing, easily pronounced, punter-proof marquee name. And no one rubbed it out. It had plainly come to stay.

Quayle grumbled and muttered that it was rather common,

and that he 'wouldn't march through Coventry with it'. (He meant that he wouldn't come into London with it – this was a reference to the ramshackle army of cripples that Pistol impresses in *Henry VI, Part II*, most of the healthy ones having bought themselves out. When Falstaff sees them he declares that though they are 'a fine body of men', he 'won't march through Coventry with them'.)

Not only did Quayle march through Coventry with it, but many years later, on his deathbed, in an unbearably moving moment, he apologized to me for the long opposition to the name, and declared that I had given him the finest part of his career and that he would be proud to march into heaven with it, if they would have him. As I bade him farewell that day, he declaimed the games–player aria he had asked me to write in the rehearsal room. I left with it ringing in my ears.

We opened the show in January 1970 at the lovely Theatre Royal in Brighton. It was a most unpropitious sleeting evening, and as we entered the theatre Michael White reminded me that I had not paid him the £1,000 investment I had been allowed in the £13,000 capitalization. (The show was in fact brought in for £11,500. Today, I have been told, it would cost nearer half a million.) There and then I wrote him out a cheque, resting it on one of the pillars of the theatre. He promptly tore it up, saying, 'Give me a quarter of that – you've been out of work for a year and have a young family to support. Don't plunge too deeply. Neither of us knows what we've got here. If the show succeeds, you will get enough from your royalties. If it fails, you will be a two–time loser.'

And so I gave him a cheque for £250.

It was meant as a friendly and protective gesture, but as the play finally made in excess of 3,000 per cent profit his gesture plainly misfired, costing me at least a couple of million pounds.

In the event, that first night was a triumph. The audience followed the convolutions of the plot like terriers and finally accorded the players a forty-five-minute standing ovation. The whole fortnight was also a triumph. Jack Tinker, then of the *Brighton Argus*, gave us a splendid review, and we were on our way, the only hiccup being a visit from Larry Olivier, who rather surprisingly gatecrashed a little party in the small bar off the stage to ask Anthony Quayle what he, as a former director of the RSC, was doing in 'a piece of piss like this'. (It was not a description he was using too prominently some years later when he accepted Quayle's role, Andrew Wyke, in the film version, nor when he received the New York Critics Award and an Oscar nomination.)

At the end of 1970 Quayle and Baxter left the St Martin's and went to America, the latter and I travelling together, suffering under the careless administrations of an air hostess whose name, Connie Newell, is etched on both our minds because of her total inability to serve us anything without spilling it. Wine, coffee, soup, gravy, ice-cream, liqueurs – all rained down on us in a constant stream of defacing liquid that gave our suits a fluid patina that Jackson Pollock would have envied.

We opened in Washington at the National Theater, and with the exception of a lone television review, thoughtfully kept from me by the remarkably caring general manager, Ben Rosenberg, we got fine notices.

Audience reaction was also enthusiastic and a grand party was thrown for us at the British Embassy by our ambassador, John Freeman, the former television producer of *Face to Face*. On arrival I thanked him profusely for the scale of the celebration, but he insisted that it was merely his job to help promote the British cause in the United States, and that he felt it a privilege to assist us, as well as a pleasure, compared to the average starchy diplomatic shindig he had normally to endure.

He also congratulated me on the tricks in the play and added that he had one of his own up his sleeve as a present for me. Leading the way up the grand marble staircase to the first floor, he ushered me into a huge darkened room, pushing me ahead of him to face a large desk with an upturned green desk lampshade, which illuminated from below a monstrous toad-like face.

'May I introduce Mr J. Edgar Hoover?' he announced suavely before swiftly retiring, leaving me alone with the most scary man in the world.

The hooded eyes were raised to mine. 'I hear you have had something of a success in the theatre,' he said slowly. Then, with added menace, he stated 'Your hero, I believe, thinks the professional police are stupid.'

'Only the English ones,' I said hastily.

'Not the G-men, then?' enquired their founder silkily, permitting himself a chilling chuckle. And then with a change of mood he suddenly snapped, 'The theatre's all you're here to do – remember that. Nothing else!'

I assured him I had no idea of doing anything else. What could he mean, etc., etc?

'You know very well what I mean, pal,' he growled. 'People come into this country – one minute they're ballet dancers, the next they're fucking defectors, spying for Uncle Joe, that sort of thing, ya know.'

I told him that as far as I knew no one in our company had any red sympathies.

'That fellow Quayle was in Albania during the war?' he asked shrewdly and correctly.

I started to talk about Quayle's wartime services but he suddenly stopped me. 'Just keep ya nose clean. I know where you're gonna be, so watch ya step.' And he named all the hotels I was booked to stay in on our tour, along with the relevant dates, together with the country addresses of a couple of close friends, plus my New York locations. It was pretty chilling that he had taken the trouble to learn so much.

'Remember,' he said in conclusion, snapping the light down off my face, 'I'll be watching. Just keep it to play-acting!'

I was dismissed. John Freeman was waiting for me in the hallway outside.

'Christ,' I said, 'he's pretty heavy!'

'I thought you would like your little present,' he replied gleefully. 'You're not the only one who can spook people out!' And he went down the stairs shaking with laughter.

Now we faced the ultimate and most fearsome hurdle – Broadway. Our producer, Morty Gottlieb, one of the most adroit producers in the business and certainly the most gluttonous – three dinners a night for him was a regular event – had booked the Music Box Theater, a charming nineteenth-century house with a stage deep enough for our beautiful set, in contra-distinction to most of the Broadway stages, which tend to be shallow and lozenge-shaped, structured to accommodate the chorus line.

The first night, set for 12 November 1970 after a week and a half of previews, was attended by many New York luminaries such as Leonard Bernstein, Stephen Sondheim, Truman Capote, Mayor Lindsay, Thomas Dewey, Joseph Heller, Rex Reed, Lillian Gish, Anita Loos, Joseph Stein and Kitty Carlisle Hart. My wife Carolyn, who had haunted the haute couture departments of Bendel's for weeks, arrived sumptuously attired in a miraculous gown of velvet and multi-coloured ribbons that Joseph himself would have envied, and we were off at last to the races.

A near flawless performance – the gun failed to shatter the ornaments in the first half, necessitating an intermission one-line dialogue change in the second act referring to bullet holes in the wall rather than signs of shattered objects – was succeeded by a grand party. In the middle of it the all-important *New York Times* arrived with Clive Barnes's stunning review, headlined 'The Best Thriller I Have Ever Seen', followed by other papers and television reviews as good as if they had just seen the Second Coming. We were a smash!

At the end of it, dazed with adulation, adrenaline and far too much booze, I very nearly ruined it all by falling down the stairs during my exit, but was mercifully saved by Carolyn's supportive arm.

And so to bed, to wake up to Morty Gottlieb on the telephone, summoning me downtown to the theatre. Not feeling so well, I tried to cry off, but he would have none of it. 'You will remember this moment all your life,' he shouted. 'I'm sending a car for you now!'

Blearily looking out of the window as we approached the theatre, I saw a line of people stretching right round the block waiting to purchase tickets. The day being freezing and wet, I asked Morty why he didn't accommodate them under the covered passage at the side of the theatre. He looked at me astounded. 'For Chrissake,' he asked, 'who would see them? If you've got it, flaunt it! As I've already indicated, Morty Gottlieb was no slouch as a producer.

The weekly magazines and Sunday reviews were equally enthusiastic, and we were off to a four-and-a-half-year run, only brought to a halt by the premature release of the movie. This oddly enough did not affect London, where we ran nearly double this length of time.

One incident at some point during the third year gave me particular pleasure. In fact I think it contained the second nicest thing ever said to me (after the words addressed to me by Agatha Christie).

I had gone to the Music Box to pick up some mail. I was about to hurry away to avoid the audience who, when recognizing one, were on occasion liable to be a trifle too physically overenthusiastic, when the stalls doors opened and out they streamed.

One woman in her late fifties, archetypically blue-rinsed and cheatered (Raymond Chandler's word for eyeglasses suspended on a chain from the neck), spotted me and homed in. I immediately denied who I was, but with my photograph in her programme she had me cold.

'Mr Shaffer,' she cried excitedly gripping my arm, 'I don't know where ya just took me, but I've never known anything like it. If my house had been burning down, and if my children had been in that house, I would not have left your theatre!'

Tears fell spontaneously from my eyes and I hugged her fervently.

'You have just made complete sense of my life,' I babbled.

'That's what we're here for.' I told her she could return as often as she liked for free – a small return for such an extraordinary life-solving remark.

The merry run at the Music Box had another extraordinary moment. One day out of performance hours, I was exploring the old theatre and had wandered right to the very top, not expecting to find much. I was admiring the wealth of gilt and curlicues when I came across a small door at the end of the passage. I found myself in the presence of what appeared to be a hundred-year-old man sitting behind a desk. He looked up at me, startled. Hastily introducing myself by way of apologizing for the intrusion, I added, 'I wrote the play here, and was just looking over the theatre. It's quite remarkable.'

'I know who you are, Mr Shaffer,' he said, 'and I know your play. I have seen it many times.'

With that he slid back a panel in the wall by his chair, revealing a clear view of the stage and auditorium many feet below. 'I hope you will be a guest here in my theatre for many years.'

'Your theatre?' I faltered, plainly enquiring who he was.

'Yes,' he said. 'I own this remarkable old pile. My name is Irving Berlin!'

With this, I have little more to say about *Sleuth* on Broadway. But what, I wondered, was going to happen next?

That was a phone call from Alfred Hitchcock. To tell the truth I had half expected it, which is almost better than not – as Elizabeth Bibesca says in *Balloons*, 'Talk about the joys of the unexpected, can they compare with the joys of the expected, of finding everything delightfully and completely what you knew it was going to be?'

7. Alfred Hitchcock

'*Modius viven*die or *viven*dee. It all depends on the college of education you attended,' said the famous dark-brown, cockney-inflected voice, thus revealing the giant scholastic chip on the semi-spherical shoulders under the inevitable funereal black cloth.

Alfred Hitchcock's question had come in response to a comment of my own on our projected working procedures to the effect that there were large holes in his pictures between the great set pieces we all knew and loved.

'Holes,' he boomed icily. 'Are you accusing me, dear boy, of being illogical?'

I realized I was just about to talk myself out of the film of Arthur La Berne's *Goodbye Piccadilly, Farewell Leicester Square* (subsequently retitled *Frenzy*), for which he had asked me to write the screenplay.

Though we were sitting in his bungalow at Universal Studios in Los Angeles, the story had really started with the phone call from Hitch to my New York apartment on New Year's Eve 1970 after the outlandish success of my play *Sleuth* on Broadway a month earlier. At first I hadn't believed that the legendary 'master of suspense' had called, assuming it to be a hoaxing friend, but, the veracity of the call having been established by the arrival of La Berne's book, I realized what a marvellous New Year's present it was. I was in very distinguished company. Among Hitch's previous screenwriters, after all, had been Raymond Chandler, Maxwell Anderson, Ben Hecht and James Bridie. In addition, this was the opportunity to work with the most prestigious man in the thriller genre.

Having flown out to the West Coast, I was now in the process of busily talking my way out of the film. The atmosphere was arctic as I blundered on. 'Yes, I suppose that's exactly what I am saying – there are huge holes in a number of your films that logically make no sense.'

'Perhaps you could give me an example of one such blighted oeuvre,' growled the maestro ominously.

'Well, in your interview with Truffaut you said *North by Northwest* was one of your favourite films.'

'I have a certain affection for the blemished work,' came the distant response. 'What of it?'

'That is one such film,' I said.

'Let us view the offending motion picture,' Hitch ground out, 'and you can enlighten me.' We repaired to the screening-room and sat side by side in fairly glacial circumstances. I'd better be right about this, I reflected apprehensively, trying to remember in detail the moment when for no very clear reason Cary Grant tries to get on the Twentieth Century train to Chicago at Grand Central Station. He is informed by the clerk, who recognizes him as a man wanted by the police, that there are no seats left but he could take the next one two hours later. He refuses and, as the clerk goes to phone the cops, storms past the platform official ticketless and on to the train. Already on it are the entire cast of villains, Eva Marie Saint, James Mason et al.

'As he has next to no reason for getting on the train, and was nearly prevented from doing so, how do they know he's going to be on it?' I asked when we reached the relevant moment.

Three hundred pounds of blubber grunted to its feet. 'Time for lunch, Tony,' it opined sepulchrally and strode from the room.

Needless to say, lunch was taken in wintry silence, but I could see that the great man was thinking furiously. At last, over the coffee, he unbent.

'Obviously, dear boy, you've never heard of the ice-box syndrome,' he said. Realizing that I had a fence or two to mend, I started on a little repair work. 'Ice-box syndrome? Oh no, I've never heard of that,' I grovelled. 'Please, tell me about it.'

'Well, it's like this,' he said. 'A bloke and his wife go and see the picture and in the middle of that night he gets out of bed and, going downstairs, takes a chicken leg from the ice-box. His wife follows him. "What's the matter Joe," she asks, "didn't I give you enough supper?" "It's not that," he replies. "I've been thinking, you know, and there's a ruddy great hole in that film," and he tells her what you've just told me. Now they fall to argufying and as a result of this they go to see the picture all over again. I've got 'em twice.' This obviously adventitious and spurious theory clearly delighted him.

'Brilliant,' I told him. 'But just how many ice-box syndromes do you want me to put into the screenplay of *Frenzy*?'

'None at all, dear boy,' was the riposte, 'just leave all that to me. Now, let's get to work.'

Face and the job were saved, and with renewed respect and amiability we moved next door to the study to commence work. This need for infallibility was to become something of a trial over the next few months, but it was greatly outweighed by his certainty.

'That's a no-scene scene,' he would say, shrewdly condemning a purely picturesque or self-congratulatory scene of purplish prose.

I must have been asked a thousand times: What was Hitchcock really like?

The answer, I suppose, is in one way very much like his often photographed public image – ponderous, lugubrious, morbid and sly. But with all this it seemed to me that he never had a clear view of his own genius. He stood much of the time in his own swollen shadow, a jester at the Court of King Alf, making bloated, fat man's films like the overblown *Notorious* and *Under Capricorn*, so sluggish that they die of inanition several times along the way.

For long passages there are no traces of the almost feminine wit of the nun's high-heeled shoes in *The Lady Vanishes*, or the one still head of the stalking murderer in the pendulum movement of the Forest Hills tennis crowd as he studies his victim in *Strangers on a Train*, or the laconic chill of 'Funny that – a plane dusting crops where there ain't no crops', said by the lone farmer on the empty road, leaving Cary Grant all alone to face his fate in *North by Northwest*.

Surprising, this last terse harbinger of doom from a man whose favourite verbal tease was to tell and retell the same stories, daring you to stop him and tell him you'd already heard it.

Fat, avuncular, deadly and a terror to actors – he once made Jon Finch apologize to the entire cast for being persistently late on set – he was nonetheless extremely kind and considerate to me. He even called me up on one occasion to ask if he could change a single word in the script.

Towards the end our relationship was somewhat soured by his biographer Donald Spoto alleging that I had said that he drank in the mornings from bottles concealed around the studio bungalow. In fact I had specifically told him there was absolutely no truth in the suggestion. If you are sitting on a sofa sharing a script, you don't have to be super-sensitive to know if your neighbour is drunk or has been drinking.

Hitch, naturally, resented this statement. Denials were useless, since you cannot prove a negative. As a result I rather spitefully withheld from Spoto the curious details of how the great man actually *did* drink – getting his secretary to add an extra ice cube to each successive drink so that there was less room for the booze and inevitably they got weaker. Months later, after a guarded rapprochement, Hitch asked me to write the screenplay of what was to be his last film, *Family Plot*, from the book *The Rainbird Pattern* by Victor Canning. The marvellous punning title, it turned out, was the only inspired thing about the entire film, and having turned it down reluctantly I came to realize I was well out of it.

In those negotiations the prosaic side of Hitch was alas uppermost. The story concerned a clairvoyant who, even though she was genuinely 'sighted', employed a shrill, or accomplice, during public performances to save her from arduous psychic labour. After all, most people just want to be told they're going to meet a tall dark stranger and will have a clutch of adorable kids, so it's best to know beforehand that they are single, childless and lucky.

Hitch wanted a wholly spurious, cheating Madame Arcarti figure without true psychic powers, riding around on a penny-farthing bicycle trailing long scarves and spouting 'that cuckoo is very angry' type dialogue. I refused point blank, and Ernie Lehman, writer of *North by Northwest*, took over. I'm very glad that he did. Compared with *Frenzy*, it was a disaster. Years later, I met Lehman at a dinner with Sam Goldwyn Jnr in La Jolla, over two dozen opened but merely sipped bottles of vintage wine. (Our host was a wine buff of great viticultural resources and largesse.) Firstly, Lehman told me that good wine was wasted on him (as it mostly is on me since I lost my sense of smell in a head operation some years ago). Secondly, he said that he was a radio ham – he in fact spent most of that evening sitting in his car in the street outside, contacting unknown dentists in New Zealand, studiously not asking them what weather conditions were like since this was information sold by the weathermen in the United States and therefore taboo. Thirdly, he informed me that working on *Family Plot* was the worst scripting experience in his life, endlessly argumentative and finally lifeless. 'You certainly knew what you were doing when you got out of that one,' he said peevishly.

All in all, it was rather sad, but I did finally take away something of considerable consequence. Hitchcock and I had virtually the same conversation about the enormous difference between a suspense story and a whodunnit as he had had earlier with Truffaut. Hitch almost never did whodunnits, the exception being *Murder*, an obscure 1930 film with Herbert Marshall.

'I generally avoid the genre,' he said, 'because they're rather like a crossword or jigsaw puzzle; there's no room for emotion.'

At the time I didn't follow that. It seemed to me one could do both simultaneously, making room for the emotion before the final revelation of identity. It was only later, when I was working with Anthony Page on *Absolution*, that I came to realize that Hitch was at least half right – that in fact there are different kinds of time engendered by audience concentration and knowledge, and if this concentration is primarily focused on who has done the murder, it vitiates and weakens everything else. It's why I believe whodunnits have always been somewhat looked down on. You have to feel for people to be concerned about them, and not only want to know their name.

There are great exceptions to this emotion/whodunnit controversy of course, *Oedipus* I suppose being the most obvious. After all, Freud ascribed to his Oedipus complex untold emotional schisms as a result of its hero's ignorance and discovery of whodunnit. He also, of course, found the first psychoanalytical archetype, later to be so convincingly expanded by Jung.

He was naturally very blinkered, as of course was Hitchcock, who knew what he did best, and what the public expected of him – pure suspense – and he stuck to it. It was the old boy's chief weakness and possibly strength; either way it gave him the certainty of the true auteur.

As Jacob Riis says in the *Author's Kalendar* of 1911, 'Men have a trick of coming up with what is expected of them, good or bad.'

8. *Sleuth* – The Film

The *Sleuth* saga moved to Pinewood in May 1972. Laurence Olivier and Michael Caine were the selected actors, Joseph Mankiewicz was the director and Ken Adam, who created the great sets on many James Bond films, was the set designer.

Caine, I might say, wasn't the first choice for Milo Tindle. That was Alan Bates – curiously enough, almost a bigger marquee name for films in those days – but he had turned us down for the most ridiculous of reasons. He had been sent to see the play by one of the producers, Morty Gottlieb, who didn't go himself. Alan, fooled by the main trick in the play at the interval, left the theatre early, thinking the part insufficient.

I got the story out of him years later at the New York Critics' Circle Awards dinner at Sardi's, when he had arrived to give a speech proposing Laurence Olivier, who had won the award. He had brought with him a sheaf of notes about the size of the London telephone directory and was very excited at the prospect of delivering it since he claimed he had never done a *proposal* speech before and had spent weeks scouring scores of dictionaries of quotations and other reference works and was highly pleased with the result.

As far as *Sleuth* was concerned, though, he was to be a two-time loser, for he was destined never to deliver it.

John Gielgud, who was to accept the award for Larry, was late. Judith Christ, the *New York Times* film critic, was hopping about like the proverbial cat on hot bricks in a tizz of anxiety because it was a live television broadcast and time was of the essence. She rushed up to me and asked whether I would accept the award on Larry's behalf, as John was a no-show. I protested that it was a bit unfair to ask me to ad lib a whole speech of acceptance when Alan had in front of him an Everest of a speech of proposal, doubtless crammed with hundreds of researched aphorisms.

'I know it's unfair, but please help me out. We really have to start now,' she said simply.

'OK, I'll do what I can, as long as you explain I'm a last-minute choice,' I agreed, already bending my mind on recalling as many jokey Larry stories as I could.

Proceedings were well under way when Judith, in full flustered flow, espied John Gielgud entering the room. She was so relieved and delighted to see him (as indeed was I!) that she stopped in her tracks and with 'And here's the marvellous Sir John Gielgud' beckoned him to the podium.

Taking this as his invitation to speak, he immediately hurried up to it, where he made the following speech: 'I'm delighted to *accept* this award on behalf of Lord Olivier. He richly deserves it as the part was so very, very difficult as to be virtually un-playable!'

He then sat down at our table, beaming benignly. 'I think that was all right?' he asked innocently.

'Absolutely,' I replied. 'Except that I'm not all that wildly happy about having *Sleuth* called unplayable, and poor Alan here is scarcely rapturous about not now being able to deliver his speech of *proposal*, which has taken him nearly a month to write, since the award has already been *accepted* by you.'

'Oh dear,' said Sir John, 'I don't suppose we could just start again, could we?'

I was now working on the screenplay in Pound Ridge with Joseph Mankiewicz when the studio (Fox) decided they wanted Caine. So we flew to Rome to talk to him.

I should mention that a certain froideur had entered our relationship, based as much as anything on Joe's unexpressed desire to write the screenplay himself (after his scripting as well as directing Oscars for *All About Eve*, this wasn't entirely unnatural). The subject of our story was of course games-playing, and one day Joe said to me, 'You know, I myself am something of a games-player.'

'Really?' I replied. 'And what is your favourite game?'

'Bilingual puns,' he said. 'That is to say, a pun in two languages.'

Thanking him cordially for the explanation, I said before I could stop myself, 'Let me see if I can play this game. Now then . . . You could say, could you not, that a man who had the reputation for being something of an aphorist but had lost it could be called a "manqué wits".'

There was a loud report as Joe bit through the stem of his pipe. His face flushed darkly, icicles formed suddenly above our heads, and his red pencil started slashing at the pages of the script.

'Geddit?' I pursued remorselessly. '"Manqué" – French for lost, and "wits", well I don't have to tell you what those are, or do I?'

He wouldn't reply. Silently I left the room, entered my limousine and was driven back to New York. Ten workless days passed without communication. Things were looking pretty grim until my agent Robbie Lantz intervened and, roaring with laughter at the story I told him, managed to patch things up. So it was that in this fragile state the pair of us set out for Rome.

Things were scarcely easier there, since Michael was very reluctant to appear with Larry in the picture.

'It would be like fighting Rocky Marciano with one hand tied behind my back,' he pleaded.

Mankiewicz assured him that he would hold the balance, saying that Caine was every bit as accomplished a screen actor as Larry, if not more so. And so it was agreed, and we moved on to Pinewood, where Ken Adam's great sets awaited us, covering two big sound stages.

Trouble struck almost at once. On the morning of the first day of shooting, I found Caine sitting in his dressing-room looking pretty unhappy. He had never met Larry, even though they had both appeared in *The Battle of Britain*, and was naturally still apprehensive of the great man, in spite of Joe's soothing reassurances.

Meeting Joe on the stage, I asked him whether he had talked to Caine yet. His gloomy stare told me that he had, whereupon I suggested a honeymoon period — if Caine and Olivier did not get on, we had no one to shoot on — so this meant no work that day, but a period in which the two men could have time to adjust to each other. After all, they were both great raconteurs and there was much to talk about and see on the stages.

'It will cost about half a million bucks,' said Mankiewicz, 'but

I guess you're right. If those two don't gel, we don't have nowhere to go.'

Things got off to a fairly chilly start when our heroes finally met.

'What do I call you?' asked Michael.

'It's quite simple,' said Larry, 'by our names – you are Mr Caine, and I am the Lord Olivier!'

Michael blanched. After a beat, Larry continued, 'That's for the first time, after which, of course, it will be Mike and Larry!'

Everyone relaxed and the day went extremely well. Jokes and anecdotes were exchanged and a lengthy champagne lunch was followed by an inspection of the sets; it seemed that the two men had settled down well together.

About five o'clock, I looked over at Joe and I drew my thumb across my throat signifying 'Let's cut it.' At this moment, of course, disaster struck.

Larry said to Michael, 'You know, dear boy, seeing you holding your head in that way, you look like the late lamented Leslie Howard.'

'Oh, 'im,' said Michael, ''e always looked as though butter wouldn't melt in 'is mouth, but I can tell you 'e 'ad all 'is leading ladies whoppo straight up,' and using his forearm and fist he made a phallic gesture.

Hell froze over. The most dangerous eyes in the business fell on the hapless Caine.

'Not, I believe,' he said sweetly, 'in *Gone With the Wind*.'

'Not, 'er, of course,' gabbled Caine, 'of course it wouldn't be 'er. Nah, there was nothing like that! . . . Not with Vivienne!'

We all scattered to the four corners of the studio, pretending to have some urgent business to attend to.

'Thanks for the honeymoon period,' Joe Mankiewicz growled at me bitterly.

Later, however, Caine seemed unaffected, even quite cheered.

'That taught me something. Never to take my eye off the old boy.'

Even later, as the shooting progressed, he came to admire him extravagantly, as indeed was the case vice versa.

Because of one of Larry's many terminal illnesses and his resentment at having been recently ousted from the National Theatre, his memory was not at its best and takes often went into the twenties and thirties. Caine, though guiltless, never by sigh nor shrug nor upturned eye evinced any sign of impatience. I remarked to him on his saintly behaviour and he replied that he was getting an acting lesson you couldn't buy.

'He never does the same thing twice,' he enthused. 'In every take he tries something new and comes at you from a new angle.'

For his part, Larry said to Caine, 'When we began I thought I had an assistant. Now I realize I have a partner.'

In the event, both men gained Oscar nominations. Alas, since they were both nominated for lead roles they unfortunately split the vote and neither won.

We did get four Oscars for the film, and I was able to say to the *New York Times*, with not wholly convincing braggadocio, that I was at least the only author who ever had had his entire cast nominated for an Oscar.

Thus finished, for the moment, the saga of *Sleuth*. And after which? 'Blessed is he who expects nothing,' said Alexander Pope to Gay, 'for he shall never be disappointed.'

9. *Murderer*

It was time to go back to the stage again, but following *Sleuth*, as you might imagine, took a bit of doing, and I'm still not quite sure that I did it with the play *Murderer*. Equally, I'm still not quite clear what exactly I did achieve, since there exist at least three different versions of the play (variously published by Marion Boyars and Samuel French); but I think I've solved it now by combining two of the versions to adduce a provocative, philosophical idea – that it is most often the victim who searches for his or her murderer, not the other way round. Basically it was an attempt to see whether it was possible to outrage and shock an audience whilst still retaining their loyalty, and to do this I used a trick of *Sleuth*ian proportions. My subject was that of a man whose sole ambition it was to become a famous murderer – not perhaps everyone's ideal – so we started with a certain amount of audience alienation.

To this I added the other fairly indigestible theory described above. I topped it off with a programme note to the effect that between them the Clean Air Acts and the street Sexual Offences Act had irreparably ruined London for tourists, since quite plainly they came to the British capital to see the fog-wreathed alleys strewn with ripped whores, and neither fog nor whores were visible today.

Michael White again bought the show, and Clifford Williams again agreed to direct. We cast Robert Stephens and Patricia Quinn (later to marry) and Caroline Blakiston and Warren Clarke.

The play began with what one reviewer called 'the most horrendous half an hour ever presented on the commercial stage', which consisted of our hero chopping up his mistress in the bath and then putting the pieces in a stove and burning them.

That there was a trick involved and a concealed purpose I have already indicated. The object was again to use the idea of spoof and gamesmanship (à la *Sleuth*) to give the hero carte blanche to murder his wife without attracting the serious attentions of the police. Of course it all goes wrong, and the true murderer/victim is finally and I hope frighteningly adduced.

We opened at the Garrick to mixed notices – some adulatory and some supercilious. I came to realize as time passed that somehow the play was not finished work and that the so-called 'sinful way to salvation' which I had intended to illustrate was still out of focus.

I was to tinker with this for years. One day I would prefer the Grecian moralistic doom-laden version as published by Marion Boyars, and then on another I would prefer the twisting, perhaps more light-weight even though equally moralistic version published by Samuel French. It was this latter which culminated in the completely revised version that was splendidly and insightfully directed by my third wife Diane Cilento at the theatre we had built in the grounds of our house Karnak in the Australian rainforest.

The curiously tepid result we achieved in London was mostly

my fault, I suppose, since it must always come back to the author to achieve what he sets out to achieve, but it was scarcely helped by Robert Stephens, whose twin obsessions with Miss Quinn and the bottle finally led him, for one performance at least, to appear almost entirely comatose.

Robert, who had served my brother Peter so magnificently as Atahualpa in *The Royal Hunt of the Sun*, once had a forty-eight-hour weekend drinking session at my house in Tregunter Road and appeared for a performance on the Monday night legless and speechless. The latter didn't matter too much for the first half an hour or so, since the passage was mute. The fact that everything was in the wrong order scarcely worried the audience, since they didn't know any better. Then matters changed dramatically when he had to speak, welcoming to his home the investigating copper, played by Warren Clarke. Firstly, he couldn't remember where the front door was, so after much knocking Warren had to let himself in. Then Warren had to feed Robert his lines; for example, 'What is your name?' became 'You are Mr Norman Bartholomew, aren't you?' This could only go on for so long, since a considerable speech or two follow the introductions. I was interested in what would happen, as Robert had previously ignored my objurgations about putting the bottle down as the weekend was over and he had a performance to give. 'I'm a professional,' he had gargled tipsily. Needless to say, I was enthralled to see what a virtually paralysed 'professional' would do. In the event he raised his eyes helplessly to the lights and crashed senselessly to the stage. The audience, again knowing no better, accepted the stage manager's explanation that 'Mr Stephens had been suddenly taken ill', and generously, as is their wont, also warmly accepted the understudy, who mercifully had not gone home. Scandal averted, we finished the show.

Michael White, on being informed of these events, was less accommodating. He felt strongly it was time to close proceedings, and so it was that we rang down our final curtain after a year. Not a happy experience, all in all. Even the poster for the show, a quartered doll-like body by the same hand that had done the masterly *Sleuth* poster of the spyglass man, was banned by the Greater London Council for God only knows what Pecksniffian reason.

The hapless and great actor continued his erratic, self-destructive course, ending with fine back-to-back performances of Falstaff and Lear and bravely facing back-to-back operations for both liver and kidney transplants, as well as earning a fully justified knighthood, before succumbing ridiculously to an urge to smoke a secret cigarette from a packet on the far side of his hospital room, and in the process falling, fracturing his shoulder, contracting pneumonia and expiring. He died as he had lived, a victim of impulse and duplicity, but wilfully and I suspect gaily – leaving a bereft and virtually penniless wife.

A film script of *Murderer* planned with the director Nic Roeg alas never took off, and this was also the fate of a New York stage performance intended to star an American/French television actor, Jean Le Clerc. Its budget was in excess of $4 million, and the suspicion was voiced by Robbie Lantz, my agent in New York, that Nic had deliberately costed it out so that he wouldn't have to face his first stage directorial assignment. This may be calumnious, but if true it was a great pity, since his ideas were quite sensational.

Whilst on the subject of Robbie Lantz, I must mention a few of the joys of having him as an agent. Not only is he vigorous and tireless in negotiation, but he gains his own way by a marvellous mix of Old World charm, bonharmonious geniality and sheer paralysing wit, of which I hope the following stories will be a sufficient illustration.

For example, when the producer Don Gregory told him that he was talking to the virtually nonagenarian Cathleen Nesbitt with a view to her playing the part of Rex Harrison's mother, Mrs Higgins, in *My Fair Lady*, Lantz murmured in his mild German accent, 'And did she answer?'

His concern about the lady's extreme age and wayward mind were fully justified on the opening out-of-town try-out. On Rex's first imperious entrance, she looked at him framed in the double doors and said with astonishment, 'Hello, Rexie. What are you doing here? I thought you were in Portofino!'

It is said he merely shook his head in total disbelief and muttering, 'We simply can't be doing with any of this!' went out into the street in full costume and make-up and took a taxi home.

Another story concerns a rather tricky meeting with the great choreographer Jerome Robbins and his legal representatives on the subject of a projected show on the former's life and work, to be entitled *An Evening with Jerry Robbins*.

To the exclusion and resentment of a number of the composers, lyricists, designers, etc., etc. who had been involved in the various shows that were to feature in the programme, Robbins's requirements concerning his printed credits grew increasingly more megalomaniac as the day proceeded. His final request was quite outrageous, being nothing less than a demand that the programme should read 'The entire production conceived by Jerry Robbins'.

This was naturally greeted by a profoundly hostile silence from the assembled company. An impasse seemed inevitable until Robbie broke it with two short sentences: 'I entirely agree, but I really must insist on the addition of one extra word: "The entire production *immaculately* conceived by Jerry Robbins".'

Needless to say, in the ensuing laughter Jerry had to concede and everything was settled amicably.

A last tale, and I think my favourite one, about Robbie Lantz is an incident when we were sitting together in the Russian Tea Room in New York.

Opposite us a preoccupied Rex Harrison was gloomily picking his way through a stack of blinis filled with soured cream and caviar when he was suddenly accosted by a self-effacing little man who shyly asked for his autograph.

Rex drew himself up and demanded in astonishment, 'Cannot you see that I'm eating my lunch?'

'But it's for my young daughter,' the man pleaded. 'She's only six and it would make her so happy if you could just . . .'

'A plague on your daughter, sir,' roared Rex. 'A murrain and a plague! Can't you see that I'm ingesting my luncheon?!'

The begging and the grandiloquent refusals continued for some time until the embarrassed, crushed supplicant lost all patience, and suddenly struck Rex lightly on the cheek with his autograph book, saying defiantly, 'Well, I really don't think she would want it anyway!'

Highly amused by the scene, Robbie Lantz murmured in my ear, 'That is the only time I have ever seen the Fan hit the Shit!'

★

I am glad to say that at the time of writing Mr Lantz, although in his late eighties, is alive and well in New York City and is as busy as ever dispersing his bons mots, sage advice and loving messages to all those lucky enough to know him.

Such is his incredible life force that I fully expect him to live to be 200.

10. The Moving Pictures

During our three years in the El Dorado building between 1970 and 1973, where Carolyn and the kids and I shared a vast apartment half a city block long, I made the acquaintance of Sam Goldwyn. Not the mogul, but his son, Sam Goldwyn Jnr. He asked me to write a script of *The Goshawk Squadron* (1971), based on the novel by Derek Robinson, a First World War story about a flying instructor squadron leader who mercilessly bullies his newly and insufficiently trained pilots to try and save their lives. Addressing them invariably as 'Mesdames', he attempts to wean them away from their public school ideals of sportsmanship and fair play.

I obliged with a suitably surreal and blackly comedic script, which though loved by Sam's writer wife Peggy found less favour with Sam himself. He was very wary of it, if not downright scared. He may have been right, claiming that the main character was too much of a monster who would completely alienate the audience, and so, the project, after many but not sufficiently softening accommodations, languished and died.

It was during my lengthy research for this film, most of it in the Imperial War Museum, that I found much practical and poignant information that came to lend a great deal of colour and depth to the story.

Typical was the fact, guessable if one reflected long enough, that, because the prevailing winds were westerly, the Allied planes always had to disengage first because of fuel problems. Their maximum speed was only a little over ninety miles an hour, and the winds on average around fifty. Thus it is easy to see that the Allied planes had to labour back to their bases at net ground speeds of about forty miles an hour while their adversaries were virtually blown home.

More emotionally, I particularly remember among a mass of documents a bloodstained scrap of paper in a notebook on which a young pilot had written to his girl: 'My darling, You have nothing to worry about. It's all going to end marvellously well. I will be home by Easter, and tell the vicar to polish up those church bells because we're going to . . .' Here the blood started.

On a less elegiac note, I also came to realize that those blithe, silk-scarved cavaliers of the sky were mostly saturated in excrement as they sat inhaling the fumes from engines lubricated by castor oil; they also needed those same scarves not so much for peacock reasons as to lubricate their necks, which constantly had to turn against the harsh material of their uniforms in order to spot enemy planes diving at them from high above and behind out of the sun and returning from below in the dreaded Immelmann turns.

This was to become very largely the pattern of my life. Literally tens if not scores of scripts lined the shelves but remained unproduced – mostly, I suspect, because of a blend of my excesses and producer timidity. I have, over the years, tended to display my disappointment with flamboyant, over-impatient behaviour. This culminated once in my hurling a water carafe down the boardroom table at the head of a major studio executive. It doesn't help in the long run – so what did I expect?!

Some of the more interesting but so far unproduced film scripts I have written include *Black Comedy* (from my brother Peter's one-act play on the interchange between dark and light – I added a blind man to this imbroglio for rather too much good measure), *Murderer* (more of this anon), and *Sting II* for Jennings Lang, the man Walter Wanger shot in the balls for tupping his wife Joan Bennett (in this – the script, not the shooting – I collaborated with Victor Spinetti and our sting was miscegenation). Despite being determined not to mention the shooting incident, I got off to a rather bad start with Jennings at Les Ambassadeurs Club. When a waiter asked him whether he wanted his vegetables on the main plate or on the side, Jennings replied, 'I like my vegetables like I like my sex, on the side.' Before I could stop myself I said, 'It does seem to me that life has taught you absolutely nothing!'

Other scripts were *Surprise Party*, for Alan Ladd Jnr and David Brown, in which a murderer is rather amusingly discovered with a corpse in his arms at a surprise party for him in his home; *Dr Jekyll and Mr Hyde*, in which Dr Jekyll turns out to be Carl Jung; *Bela Lugosi* for a producer at Fox of particularly opaque intellect called Michael Levy, who could make nothing of a highly inventive script crammed with splendid wheezes, though I say so as what shouldn't; *Masada*, for a charming producer described to me by a friend as 'small but perfectly formed', Joseph Shaftel, though unfortunately in this I made the Roman besiegers the heroes rather than the embattled Zealots, to the chagrin of the Israeli government; *Citizen of the World*, a life of Charlie Chaplin, which was trumped by the Attenborough film; and *A Great Reckoning in a Little Room*, a four-part TV series commissioned by the BBC, a run-around thriller which inter alia proved that Christopher Marlowe wrote as Shakespeare, and which was entirely unappreciated by an American producer called Beth Porter and a temporarily unapproachable head of drama who at the time appeared to me and most of his staff to be having a nervous breakdown.

Another calamitous exercise was a spoof spy story set in the Windmill Theatre in Second World War London for Lisa Minelli, axed by boy producers at Warner Brothers, who didn't know the genre, but is worth recording for a redoubtable run-in with Frank Sanatra at a theatre on Long Island, some considerable distance from New York City.

My producers (and not surprisingly the original producers of *I Am A Camera* suggested I see Minelli live on stage. She was currently doing a three-handed cabarat with Sinatra and Sammy Davis Jnr which certainly promised an evening of delight. And so it was that we made the long journey out to the Island to see the show, full of a keen anticipation which alas was to be cruelly disappointed. On arrival, Lisa told us there would be no show as Frankie had a cold.

'Couldn't you and Sammy do the show without Frank?' I asked her. After all they were both considerable cabaret artistes.

'I don't think Frankie would like that very much,' she quavered in a frightened voice.

'Perhaps I'll go along the passage and try and persuade him,' I ventured.

She blanched. 'Are you plum crazy?' she asked. 'You don't know what you're messing with.'

It was quite obvious that he was running the whole show and that she was deathly scared of him.

'It seems a bit unfair to let all these people come all the way out here and then announce the cancellation,' I persisted.

'That's how it is,' she replied urgently. 'Now leave it alone.'

'But if I just reasoned with him . . .'

'For Chrissake leave it alone,' she repeated, nervously looking towards her partly opened dressing-room door which had stirred slightly.

From behind it suddenly came the well-known gravelly voice of Sinatra.

'The little ladys right. If Frankie don't sing, nobody sings,' it said ominously. 'And if I were you, I'd beat it right now. Unless that is you want a little welcoming party waiting for you when you get back to suite 501 of the Plaza Hotel where I believe you are staying.'

This so nearly replicated J. Edgar Hoover's performance in the British Embassy in Washington that I almost laughed out loud. Lisa wisely restrained me. She was quite clearly a terrorized, caged, songbird singing to the tune of 'Ol' Blue Eyes'.

I also had trouble in Ireland working on a TV series of Frederick Forsyth's *The Negotiator*, and an earlier story would probably explain why. I had sent a note over to Fred Zinnemann in the restaurant at Pinewood stating that I had a better ending to the film of *The Day of the Jackal*, which he was directing, than Forsyth. Zinnemann sent a note back with a question mark on it. I sent one back stating boldly $50,000. He replied with a terse comment to the effect that the book had sold a trillion copies with the ending already written (de Gaulle going to the old soldiers' parade and giving the double kiss which the Jackal hadn't reckoned on, shooting and missing and being arrested). He would stay with that.

The completed film was not the great success the book had been, and eighteen months later I bumped into Fred outside his apartment in Mount Street.

'Herr Shaffer,' he said, buttonholing me, 'what was all that business in the commissary at Pinewood about you having a better end to the *Jackal*?'

I looked meaningfully across the road to the Connaught Hotel. 'Do you know what that building is over there?' I asked insouciantly.

'Of course! It's the Connaught Hotel,' he replied shortly.

'They do the best lunch in London,' I stated, staring him straight in the eye.

'All right,' he sighed. 'I'm a punter!'

And arm in arm we crossed the road. At the table no mention was made of the ending. Vast quantities of expensive food and pre-phylloxera claret were consumed, and still I kept silent and to his credit, gallantly, so did Fred, at least on the relevant subject. At length over a priceless bottle of Dow's '28 port, he finally lost his patience.

'So?!' he asked peremptorily.

'What,' I asked with some stateliness, 'was the main problem with the book *The Day of the Jackal*?'

'It was, of course, that everyone knew that de Gaulle was not assassinated,' he replied.

After a dramatic pause, I said, 'How did they know?'

A shadow passed across the great director's face.

'I think I see where you are going,' he responded flatly.

'I thought you would. It's really quite simple. In the book, the police inspector, who has bird-dogged the Jackal's footsteps quite brilliantly and knows he is in Paris, tries vainly to persuade de Gaulle not to go to the old soldiers' parade. In my version, *apparently* de Gaulle takes his advice and it's agreed a double will be sent. We retain Forsyth's trick of the kiss and then, having missed, the Jackal calmly reloads and blows the man's head off. He then escapes to his London flat, where we next pick him up.

'As in the existing film, the Jackal is surrounded by blow-ups of balloons and papier mâché heads of de Gaulle. No one – not even Madame de Gaulle – knows his face better. The Jackal is studying a copy of *The Times* in which a photograph shows the French President waving from a balcony of the Elysée Palace; the headline reads "De Gaulle's Double Assassinated at Old Soldiers' Parade".

'Or is it the French President?! With a magnifying glass and callipers, the Jackal is carefully examining the face in the photograph. He soon realizes that scars and birthmarks are marginally in the wrong position. This is the double on the balcony. He has shot the real de Gaulle and thus is entitled to his second half of his million-dollar fee from the OAS.

'All through the film we have wanted an honourable draw between the Jackal and the inspector, because they have both been so adroit. So now the police inspector enters, sees the evidence and realizes that the Jackal understands all – that in fact the Fourth Republic is now being led by a non-entity, the de Gaulle lookalike.

'He tells the Jackal, "We're even. The wonderful chase is over. You're free to go. But tell no one. If you try and go for the second half of your money, I'll take you out of the game permanently."

'What do you think?' I asked. 'Was it worth the lunch?'

Zinnemann was thunderstruck, 'I wish I had bought it at Pinewood,' he said. 'It's wunderbar. It answers everything!'

We crossed the road to Fred's flat. As he walked up the steep flight of stairs, I asked him whether he was going to tell Forsyth.

He looked down at me from the top and said trenchantly, 'Would you?'

But he did. And thus originated the later difficulty of my working with Forsyth. To return to *The Negotiator*, with my three bosses all putting their two cents' worth in, after ten weeks we hadn't reached agreement on the first quarter of the first episode. As there were thirteen episodes in the series, I could easily see that I would never live to leave Dublin. So I walked round the corner from my rented flat off the Ballsbridge Road (incidentally overlooking a women's cricket club) and somewhat reluctantly returned to Radio Telefis Éireann three-quarters of my fee and quit the Emerald Isle.

Another unproduced film made me quite improbably the partner of the incomparable ballet dancer Baryshnikov. This brief corybantic career was launched unwittingly by Jon Peters, the ex-hairdresser, producer friend of Barbra Streisand, who asked me to get involved with the scripting of a film inspired by the murder of a young lead orchestral viola player whose strangled and raped body had been found in an elevator shaft during intermission at a concert at the Met in New York (incidentally the culprit – a scene shifter – was found because he had used a knot only used by members of his profession).

I suggested a change from orchestral concert to ballet on the grounds that it was obviously much more visual. Peters agreed. And so it was that I found myself in the company of the Director of the American Ballet Company flying out to Los Angeles to meet and study at work his company, now led by Baryshnikov, who had recently defected from Russia.

At the first training session, which had lasted all morning and appeared to me to be the workout from hell, I was thankful to be able to just sit and observe. But in the afternoon things changed dramatically.

'You can't really understand enough just watching,' said Baryshnikov, 'you must join in!'

I looked pretty dubious, having the flexibility of Michelangelo's *David*, but he was insistent.

'Come and stand by me and try some of the exercises. I'll tell you which ones to do. Don't dream of trying any of the others – you'll put yourself in hospital!'

With the greatest possible trepidation I did as bid, and I might say even the 'easy' exercises I was allowed were something out of Torquemada's torture chamber. I even assayed a simple two-step culminating in a modest jeté. At the more than welcome end of the session, Baryshnikov was full of praise for my 'gallantry', as he put it, and seizing me in an iron bear-hug towed me off into a repeat of it to the plaudits of the company.

Thus for a few brief moments I became Baryshnikov's partner! With a few more practices he assured me charmingly I would be ready to be his number two, a position currently held by a giant carthorse of a dancer called Gudinov, who had defected with him and whom he also assured me was a Soviet spy sent to keep an eye on the company to prevent further defections.

I have been lucky in my life to have worked with a number of the world's legendary (read Hollywood) film directors – Hitchcock, Mankiewicz, Wilder – yes, the incomparable Billy Wilder (*Some Like It Hot, Double Indemnity, Sunset Boulevard, Witness For the Prosecution, The Seven-Year Itch, The Apartment, The Long Goodbye, Ace in the Hole*, etc., etc.), though alas I never filmed with him. Many conversations, projects, but no completed work. Wilder had once said that he wanted to collaborate with me instead of his regular scripting partner I. A. L. Diamond on his next film after *Buddy Buddy*, but alas he never made one.

I met him first at a lunch in the company of America's favourite and most successful jockey, Willie Shoemaker (aka 'the Shoe'), and I asked him whether he would consider directing my play *Murderer* on the Broadway stage. Naturally he asked to read it before committing himself.

In the event *Buddy Buddy*, a film he had just completed, having opened to disastrous reviews, settled the matter. He couldn't leave Hollywood because he thought he was now an outcast and his whole career a total failure. (But in the book *Conversations With Wilder*, by Cameron Crowe, he claimed rather perversely, in answer to a question about whether he had ever been blissfully happy, that the only day of bliss in his life was when, after a lousy preview opening, even the studio guard looked away as he came in. For the moment, he was free of the Hollywood machine.)

Unbelievably, he had never directed a stage play and wasn't about to start now, after a movie flop, which shows the quite incredibly unforgiving nature of a society that could, he believed, say to its oldest and most accomplished son, 'You're only as good as your last picture.' Incidentally, he has never been allowed to direct again!

He did, however, give me invaluable advice about the structuring of my play, for no one was ever more knowledgeable about this most important of all aspects of storytelling.

'What's your most climactic scene?' he asked.

I mentioned it, and he said, 'Yes! That's it! Then what's all this other shit that comes after it?!'

'That's the philosophical content of the piece,' I replied defensively.

'Philosophy. Schmilosophy! You've got it in the wrong place. Once you've done that scene, bring the goddamn rag [curtain] down!'

He was of course absolutely right. I'll leave you with two other remembrances of him by way of thanks.

The first is so often repeated that it is probably apocryphal. A young but untried whippersnapper producer with a two/three picture deal at one of the major studios, probably purchased for him by a fond papa, asked Billy to lunch. He began with almost certainly the most impertinent question he could ask.

'Excuse me, Mr Wilder, but could you please tell me about yourself. I mean, what exactly have you done?'

Wilder, always the soul of politesse, courteously cut his head off with a sad, but forgiving smile.

'Of course,' he said, 'but you first!'

The second I can vouch for personally. Wilder and I had

agreed to meet at the *downtown* Brown Derby (Durby in local parlance), as distinguished from its fellow restaurant *uptown* in Beverly Hills.

Atypically, he arrived some twenty minutes late, full of apologies. He was spitting tacks and recounted the following reason for his lateness. He had a simple scene to shoot ten minutes before the lunch break and two bit actors from Central Casting had been sent to play the parts of a couple of hoodlums in a bar. The dialogue they had to speak was of the very simplest:

ıst HOOD:

OK, tomorrow night Joey gets it.

2ND HOOD:

I can't do dat. Joey is my bruvver.

ıST HOOD:

What's the matter – scruples?

After lengthy discussion about their motivation (BW: 'Your extremely overgenerous pay packets'), they finally settled to do the scene just as they were about to pull the lights. This went as follows:

ıST HOOD:

OK, tomorrow night Joey gets it.

2ND HOOD:

I can't do dat. Joey is my bruvver.

ıST HOOD:

What's the matter, **S**cruples?

'He thought Scruples was the man's name,' explained Billy. 'This is the kind of shit they are sending up from Central Casting today! Of course we never got the shot!'

Finally, I think I can do no better than to list Wilder's tips for writers:

1. The audience is fickle.

2. Grab 'em by the throat and never let 'em go.

3. Develop a clean line of action for your leading character.

4. Know where you're going.

5. The more subtle and elegant you are in hiding your plot points, the better you are as a writer.

6. If you have a problem with the third act, the real problem is in the first act.

7. A tip from Lubitsch: 'Let the audience add up 2 + 2. They'll love you for ever.'

8. In doing voice-overs, be careful not to describe what the audience already sees – add to what they are seeing.

9. The event that occurs at the second act curtain triggers the end of the movie.

10. The third act must build, build, build in tempo and action until the last event and then –

11. That's it – don't hang around.

They're easy enough to understand, but not quite so easy to put into practice.

After a great director, a great producer. A couple of stories about the mega-mogul, Sam Spiegel (*Lawrence of Arabia*, *The African Queen*, *On the Waterfront*, *Doctor Zhivago*, etc., etc.).

One day he invited me to his New York apartment on Park Avenue which more closely resembled the Roman forum than a modern habitation – artfully broken marble columns and busts littered a vast expanse of cracked marble flooring. The walls, incongruously, were festooned with Cézannes, Monets, Manets, Modiglianis, Bonnards and Van Goghs bought, he told me once, perhaps to emphasize his perfect taste rather than his crassness, at a time when the Tate and National Galleries had none of them.

My brother, Peter, was having difficulties collaborating with the renowned stage director Peter Brook on a screenplay of Golding's *Lord of the Flies* which he, Spiegel, had commissioned, and I suspected rightly that it was because of this that I had been invited.

When I arrived there was no sign of Sam in the vast Ancient World replica, and the only reading matter was a copy of *Newsweek* prominently displayed on a huge coffee table and opened at a page headlined 'The mystery of the missing Degas bath studies.' It appeared that half a dozen Degas sketches of young ladies clambering into and out of bathtubs had gone walkabout in suspicious circumstances.

Suddenly the vast bronze doors opened reverberatingly and the great man was with me – tiny, rotund, and twinkling apologetically for his tardiness at me over his then quite illegal Havana Corona Corona.

I pointed out the *Newsweek* article, saying, 'That's some mystery, eh, Sam?'

'Com vith me!' he said imperiously in his thick Mittel-European accent, and led the way to a sunken marble bathroom some dozen or so steps below us. Round the walls hung the six Degas bath studies! 'Zo you see,' he said, beaming triumphantly 'zere ees no mystery!'

A second story shows the guile of Mr Spiegel. When the Nazis were in power they banned all films in Germany credited to Jewish producers. Sam changed his name on his films to S. P. Eagle. Even to this day, you can still see on some of them – 'Produced by Sam Spiegel (the former S. P. Eagle)'! It may have been an act of duplicity but it certainly was better than bankruptcy.

A second great producer almost equal and opposite to Sam Spiegel was of course Joseph E. Levine (*A Bridge Too Far, Hercules*, etc.).

Another short, powerhouse Munchkin, he employed me to write a screenplay for *The Glow*, a spooky novel somewhat in the style of *Rosemary's Baby*, though stylistically or imaginatively not in the same class as the Ira Levin book. Both employed a group of apparently normal, neighbourly, people who had other completely secret hidden agendas. In *Rosemary's Baby* they were Satanists; in *The Glow* they were centenarians disguised as youthful joggers, and health freaks. The trouble with *The Glow* is that it went nowhere; it shook hands with itself. Once you knew the secret – that was it. And until you knew it nothing much happened at all.

Anyway, I undertook to solve the problem, and with Joe's generous help took up residence in Trump Tower, a prestigious and alarmingly clever apartment block on midtown Fifth Avenue affording a view uptown over the whole of nocturnally no-go Central Park to no-go-at-anytime Harlem and downtown to the vasty towers of the Trade Center, and between them St Patrick's Cathedral, golden-top roofs of the 20s and 30s, Saks Fifth Avenue, and the perennial clutch of Irish doormen lounging on the sidewalks.

The astonishing thing about Trump Tower was the cunningly arranged windows which prevented one apartment from seeing into another, but at the same time allowing all to have the same unique plutocratic view!

Joe himself never interfered with the work and seldom asked about it, but insisted on a weekly lunch meeting at the oligarchic and beautiful Four Seasons whose wallpaper and decor changed with them. There a strange ritual would take place. The maître d' would appear and announce the special dish of the day — say for example sautéed scrod, and Joe would ask him whether he was allowed to eat it. The maître would feign bewilderment and Joe would say, 'Go call my wife and ask her whether I am allowed scrod.'

The man would dutifully go to the phone and pretend to call Mrs Levine 100 miles or so away, and then come back with the illusory answer depending largely I suspect on what dish the restaurant wanted to sell. If he said, 'No, unfortunately your wife forbids it,' Joe would invariably order a large portion of it. If he said, 'Yes, she thinks it will be very good for you,' Joe would equally inevitably ask, 'What's your second special today?' and of course order it. Not a lunch ever passed without this lunatic tennis being played.

He sat every day at the same table on the south side of the great fountain in the dining room, staring intently out of the window at the opposite end of it. I asked him once why he did this and he replied with deadly seriousness, 'I like to keep an eye on my bank!' I laughed but he was surprised. 'It's good for the digestion seeing people going in and out of that open door. One day during the crash of 1929 I showed up at my bank and it was closed with all the shutters pulled down.' I agreed that it wouldn't have been a very digestible sight.

After lunch he would ask me to stroll the avenue with him and so we would proceed arm in arm up either Fifth or Park. On the steps of the Four Seasons, the same pantomime would be repeated with me as with the maître d' inside. 'Is it cold or do I need the fur?' he would ask. If I said it was cold he would throw the coat into the back of the half-a-block-long black limousine that awaited him, or if I said the reverse he would wear it, shuffling along under its impossible weight followed by the ominous overblown car, travelling obediently behind him at under half a mile an hour.

In the end he employed an ancient Hollywood hack called Red to judge the script, and his uncomprehending assessment stalled the project. By the time we had got it all sorted out, Joe had died suddenly, and equally uncomprehending, but not before he had contributed an insulting and acrimonious conversation in his office about an owed cheque for $25,000 with my agent, Robbie Lantz, who behaved in such a dignified and calm way in the face of strictures that he, Lantz, was a squalid dun, that he forced the shamed Levine to chase after him down the corridor outside his office waving the required cheque in palliating surrender. I wish that hadn't been my last sight of the Monstre Sacré but it was probably fitting.

Morris West asked me to do a screenplay of a book of his called *The World Is Made of Glass*. The story is laid out in chapters alternately named Magda and Jung. Magda is a sexual sadist who is spinning out of control and who seeks psychiatric help from Jung. The trouble is that the trashy Magda is exalted and that the exalted Jung is trashed (he even ejaculates in his pants whilst analysing Magda!). Rix Weaver, the leader of the Carl Jung Society, begged me not to represent the great man in the calumnious way that Morris West had done and I agreed. Morris was seriously underpleased when he eventually read the script.

'You must give more emphasis to Magda and less to Jung,' he said furiously. 'We have had many hundreds of letters about Magda, and none about Jung.'

'That,' I said tartly, 'is because the public is pruriently inclined, and simply cannot cope with truly great men – as you can't!'

'You can do this script as I want it,' he fumed.

'Certainly I can,' I replied, 'but I will not! You have turned a giant into a pygmy.'

And that was that.

If I seem overly cantankerous, I must point out in my own defence that none of the film subjects I have detailed were ever actually made with another writer.

Among the unmade films is a script penned by me in 1997 about the great Turkish leader, Atatürk, for Larry Olivier's son, Tarquin. I was duplicitously replaced by him behind my back by another writer, when he found he couldn't afford my contracted rewrites, even though he had wept with joy on the telephone when he had first read it. The film I suspect never will be made. Tarquin, is, I fear, seriously hobbled by his obsessive worship of his father. An impossible act to follow!

I also wrote a screenplay of Wilkie Collins's *The Moonstone* for David Picker, whose favourite book he claimed it to be. He assured me that he would produce it just as soon as he became head of Paramount, which was upcoming. He duly became head of Paramount and totally unacknowledged it – so what did you expect?!

All these aborted efforts may subconsciously be connected with my very first visit to the cinema, which was not an auspicious one. It took place when I was about five years old in the Scala flea-pit in Liverpool. In those days, of course, there was no television in our house, so I was completely ignorant of what a moving picture with synchronized sound might be (as indeed was a high percentage of the population in 1931, I suspect).

When I first beheld in almost total darkness a gigantic silver human being, apparently talking almost directly at me but not in any way acknowledging my waves and even shouted responses, I became terrified and hid behind the circle balustrade, and no amount of maternal coaxing would induce me to emerge again and face the horrifying apparition.

I am not at all sure that I've completely got over it even to this day, though terror has been replaced by mesmeric surrender. And in a back-handed way, I suppose, familiarity is the enemy of expectancy.

11. *Absolution* and Three Plays

I finally got a producer, Elliott Kastner, interested in producing a film of mine, *Absolution*, which had taken ten years to get made. He was a cleanliness freak who had an office at Pinewood Studios together with a quirky, though as far as I was concerned ineffectual, Irishman called Danny O'Donovan. Elliott's chauffeur told me one day that he had once been sent from Windsor to the London apartment at two o'clock in the morning to clean an ashtray of one cigarette butt and plump a cushion.

Originally called *Play with a Gypsy*, among other abortive adventures suffering from a fractured handshake deal with Alan Ladd Jnr, it was a twisted tale of the torture of a priest by a crippled boy who is jealous of another boy, the former's favourite. Eventually, by using the device of the confessional, he induces him to commit murder.

These three roles were in the end to be played by Richard Burton, Dai Bradley and Dominic Guard, a fine enough cast calamitously directed by Anthony Page, who at one time had his boyfriend secretly reworking my script behind my back. No reasonable man, by which I mean that definition as per English law, the man on the Clapham omnibus, would ever have allowed this fellow to write the bus tickets on the omnibus, let alone the script of a complex feature film!

It was bad enough having a drunk for a leading man, let alone a director who was too much of a wimp even to print let alone use his overtheatrical takes on the rare occasions when he managed to remember enough of the lines actually to complete them.

But Page's most heinous mistake was to ignore a vital suggestion of mine out of sheer arrogance. The deus ex machina was the confessional box itself. In it you cannot be seen and can only be heard in a whisper − obviously a form of verbal communication that lacks vocal colour. This makes it easy for one boy to impersonate another and confess to wholly illusory circumstances and blame them on him.

Halfway through making the film, I realized that it would be much more terrifying for the audience to know what was really going on, how in effect the priest was being slowly conned into murdering one of his charges. To this end, I suggested to Page that during a break in filming we use the time to shoot Dai Bradley in the little box confessional set, rising from his knees by the partition, walking to the door, half opening it, giving us a sly look, closing it again as if he had exited and then resuming his place by the partition, thus at a stroke persuading the priest he was another boy and tipping the wink to us. The set was already lit and Bradley was in costume, but Page refused to do it.

'You should have thought of that before,' he said.

It was useless to point out that I had thought of it in time and its inclusion disturbed none of his future shooting plans but merely gave him an option he might come to miss later.

And this he duly did, at the first rough assembly, when an invited audience of studio cleaners and anyone around who didn't know the plot said as one that they all wished they had known the plot earlier and not received it in a gabbled-off speech at the end of the last reel. It was too late to reshoot, because Dai Bradley had that morning flown to South Africa and the producer was unwilling to spend any further money. I don't know what, if anything, Page learned from the incident, but I at least learned that not all thrillers are whodunnits to be revealed at the very end.

Another thing I learned at that time was never to trust the longevity of hellraiser film stars. I had taken a bet with Richard Burton that he would never play King Lear on Broadway. I had suggested a stake of £1,000 but because, as he put it, 'world stars don't play for peanuts', he upped it to $250,000.

That same afternoon he was visited in his caravan by the suits from Broadway to discuss the production.

After a couple of hours, they left disgruntled, leaving behind an outraged Burton.

'Do you know, boyo,' he said in his Welsh accent, 'they wanted me to play it eight times a week. They must be crazy. No one plays Lear eight times a week.'

I told him that Wolfit had, but, said Burton, he was just another crazy.

Even so, I pointed out, eight performances or not, he still wasn't going to play Lear on Broadway, which was the substance of our bet; he owed me the quarter of a million. He grunted gloomily, but unfortunately the man was summoned to the great Casting Director in the Sky before he got around to paying it!

In the event *Absolution* finally opened at the Lane Cinema in

St Martin's Lane with a six-week season and to respectable if comparatively unexcited reviews.

The Wicker Man and *Sommersby* followed. In the latter I had a curious credit, 'from an idea by', which put me in mind of the well-known Danny Kaye pattersong: the two have one thing in common – in neither film does the cavalry come. This lack of a happy ending produces horror in the first one, and hankies in the second, *Sommersby* having been called a five-Kleenex job. Its only interest was for me to pose an interesting amatory dilemma – in the courtoom, if the suspect Richard Gere character answers, 'Yes,' to the heroine Jodie Foster's question 'Do you love me?' he instantly condemns himself to death. It was intended to have the same self-immolating effect as Sydney Carton's 'far, far better thing'. In its somewhat tawdry way I think it did.

The producer was Arnon Milchan. Though we didn't always see eye to eye, I must say of him that at first he appeared to be one of the few film producers who actually pay one what is owed without having to be chased. Later I was to discover differently, and he joined the majority of the others who, if they behaved the same way in any other business, would mostly be in jail for fraud. It is the claim of a leading debt investigation and collection agency that they have never yet failed to find money owing from the major film production companies to a client who has asked them to look into the matter. The delightful name of this agency is Solomon and Finger!

On the whole, however, I prefer the stage to the film studio. The author is more respected and has more control, and the

Victorian colloquialism 'before your very eyes' is still as true today as ever it was in the face of the huge challenge of screen shadow. In spite of all the new astounding special effects and animatronics etc., etc., you can still astound more in the playhouse than in the movie house. When you can do everything, the audience tends to believe less and less, and you will increasingly find that you can actually achieve less and less. In the theatre, audiences, I believe, expect less and almost certainly are liable to get more than they expect.

12. *The Wicker Man* and Diane Cilento

After a painful divorce from Carolyn in 1984, my new uxorious partner was a luminous Australian actress and savant previously married to Sean Connery.

We had met as a result of my seeking to cast *The Wicker Man*, a quirky film examination of the nature of sacrifice and Celtic mythology, penned for a consortium consisting of Peter Snell, the managing director of British Lion, and Christopher Lee, the horror movie star.

After a false start, when on my suggestion we had all bought a cinematically useless book called *Ritual*, I had been constrained to write an original in its place instead of giving them their money back. 'You don't get out of this so easily,' said Snell. 'I want a screenplay from you.'

So I asked myself what were the constituent elements of Celtic sacrifice. This seemed to me to be that the victim had to be (a) king for a day, (b) come willingly to the sacrifice, and, most importantly, (c) be a virgin. Thus armed with this abstract, I fitted up the plot of *The Wicker Man*, which got its name from a monstrous wicker figure ritually filled with sacrificial animals, and Edward Woodward into the bargain.

Edward played the lead, an investigating copper from the mainland who comes to Summerisle, the pagan domain of the laird, played by Christopher Lee. Edward performed quite beautifully, with the greatest patience, subtlety and fortitude, no mean feat when you are in glacial conditions in practically every shot (though miraculously almost every day the sun shone on our enterprises, in Gulf Stream coastal country, while ten miles away blizzards raged).

Christopher Lee's performance was also remarkable – powerful, terrifying and, at times, lunatic, as he pranced about as the sinister 'teaser' to the Hobby Horse in his mauve pleated frock and long fright wig. He believed it was the best script he ever did, and has often said as much!

Stuart Hopps of the Scottish National Ballet did our excellent primitive choreography, and Paul Giovanni, a great friend of my brother Peter, composed a truly awe-inspiring first film music track, much of it scored for Scottish fiddles and brass band, concluding with an arrangement of 'Summer Is Icumen In' to rival Benjamin Britten's.

If in this case somewhat improbably cast, the always original Lindsay Kemp gave us a dotty innkeeper, and the three blondes we had decided on were Diane Cilento, Britt Ekland and Ingrid Pitt.

The former, who was to become my wife, I found in a strange farmhouse in Sherston near Malmesbury, Wiltshire. I had sent her the script after intially being deterred by her agent, Jimmy Fraser of Fraser and Dunlop, who told me she had left the business and gone back to school. I was determined to find her, having seen her on the stage in Giradoux's *Tiger at the Gates*, and needing to balance out Ingrid and Britt.

The farmhouse was strange because it contained, in place of normal domestic appurtenances, half a dozen packing cases, her small son Jason and a jug of home-made damson wine. And that was it. Hardly the trimmings of a film star, a job I was to learn later that she held in some contempt, having been through the Bond experience with her then husband Sean Connery.

I asked her about the nature of the school that she had attended, and she told me that it was run by John Godolphin Bennett, a disciple of the great philosopher and magus, George Ivanovitch Gurdjieff. Mr B., as Mr Bennett was called, was himself later to play a significant part in the lives of myself and my previous wife, Carolyn, as a teacher, friend and guide at Sherborne House in Gloucestershire. As for Diane, after all the glitz and vacant razzmatazz of showbiz she had wanted to find some answers to the fundamental questions: Who are we? Why we are here? Where we are going, if anywhere? etc., etc.

'And did you find them?' I asked her.

'I'll tell you in Scotland,' she answered, thus obliquely telling me that she liked and accepted my script.

To command this disparate band, I had decided that our director should be Robin Hardy. He had been my partner in the commercial film company Hardy Shaffer and Associates, and his wife at the time, Caroline, assured me that he had a heart condition that necessitated a peaceful and contemplative way of life, so I asked him to do some research background on Celtic mythology, abundantly available from the public library in Maidenhead, as they had gone to live nearby on a tiny island in a fork on the River Thames. The resulting film was in some ways relatively unimaginative, showing some evidence of inexperience, with quite a few sequences of clichéd haste; Robin's inability to work harmoniously with either his art director Seamus Flannery or the veteran cameraman Harry Waxman, cost us dear. Even so, he managed to assemble a highly original movie.

We were much further damaged by the new managing director at British Lion, Michael Deeley, who, in the hallowed tradition of studio bosses disowning their predecessors' pet projects and burying them, freely proclaimed his hatred of the film, 'the worst film I've seen in ten years'. He had it hacked to bits, even going so far, it has been said, to immure cans of out-takes under the M3, and finally put it out almost as a B-movie on a double bill with Nic Roeg's *Don't Look Now*. In all fairness, I should point that the film was painstakingly and lovingly reconstituted to something approaching its desired length by Robin some months later, working from odds and ends of dupe negative with the greatest possible patience and persistence. Without this I don't believe that it would have survived to gain its currently exalted cult status.

The above depredations did not prevent it from winning major prizes at film festivals, notably the highly prestigious Grand Prix of the Festivale de Filmes Fantastiques in Paris (in the case of the Oxford festival, where it beat out Peter Brook's *Meetings With Remarkable Men*, no awarded statuette was ever sent to me, though it was promised), nor did they prevent it from being picked up by the kids at UCLA in California and in many other cities to become a huge cult success, and it was adopted by The *Wicker Man* Appreciation Society, an oddball crew of enthusiasts in America. The film now lives on, the celebrated prey of film journalists, BBC documentaries and horror movie enthusiasts. A group of devoted acolytes are even now putting out their own *Wicker Man* fanzine in Scotland. In addition there was the novelization by Hardy and me, recently reissued and a splendidly relevatory book on the making of the film by Alan Brown, the Scottish Journalist of the Year, called *Inside the Wickerman*. In short *The Wicker Man* has been called The *Citizen Kane* of horror movies – and that is praise enough!

During the ten-week shooting of the film, Diane and I started an affair. When it came for her to leave the Scottish location, which was earlier than me, she left me two things – her address in Wiltshire and a copy of *Beelzebub's Tales to His Grandson* (the first in the *All and Everything Series*) by Gurdjieff, telling me I wouldn't understand a word as it was written in his own code. Linguistically, he was a jack of all languages and a master of none. *Heptaparaparshinokh* is a word for electricity, *hamblazoin* for the essence that coats the soul, *exiohari* for the sperm and *vibroechonitanko* is remorse.

I had become fascinated by these teachings, even though incompletely understanding them, and I was also intrigued that a world star had, as it were, given up the trappings and glitter of showbiz fame for the contemplative life.

That Diane had worked hard and had become an adept was beyond doubt to me as she unfolded her experiences over glasses of the Big GM as we called Glenmorangie, the single-malt whisky we had selected to exclude the cold on the draughty location. More and more, I came to realize that this wasn't just a love affair but was also an invitation to enter a door to genuine spiritual enlightenment and the real possibility of transformation. That the two were interlinked, there was no question. As we all know, new love affairs can be compulsively beguiling, so I had to ask myself seriously whether my interest in the latter was not a spurious cloak for my interest in the former.

Diane found no antipathy in the dichotomy – finding the Way to the Source was an act of love – and she promised on my firm request to introduce me to Mr Bennett.

I soon drove from Scotland down to England, debating as I did so whether or not to go to Scott's Farm, Diane's home, and become seriously embroiled, or to consider my marriage and Carolyn and our two children and stop in time.

I had reached a crossroads, mentally and physically, since I suddenly found myself locked in this rumination literally at a crossroads in my car in the depths of the countryside; one road led to London and my family, and the other to Wiltshire and to Diane. After what seemed like days I chose the latter and drove joyously towards what awaited.

The appointment with Mr Bennett wasn't long in materializing. For the first couple of days Diane and I had tramped the magical fields of the local estate, discussing, apart from our own preoccupations, *Goshawk Squadron*, the film I was then writing. But I soon found myself in an ice chamber in Sherborne House facing a thin, gaunt man in his mid-sixties, who spent the first twenty minutes of our meeting furiously poking a sullen and reluctant coal fire. As Mr Bennett had at one time been head of the Coal Board, I ventured my surprise that someone with this history should be apparently so unfamiliar with the combustible properties of fossil fuel. He seemed somewhat unresponsive to this, but presently arose from the floor to deliver himself of a lengthy discourse on General Slim, a man I knew nothing about whatsoever. With that he bade me a fond goodbye, and I left, much perplexed.

Later I was to come to know that his obliqueness of manner concealed a shrewd character evaluation that he was conducting,

and this was interspersed with an alarming directness character-
ized by flashes of his piercing blue eyes and terse statements.

Sometime later, as we drove along in my car towards Burford
(mercifully I was driving – he was a horrendous driver, his head
always in deep contemplation or fierce abstruse examination),
he said to me, 'You know, in your case, even the lightest touch
on the reins would suffice.'

I am afraid I was, I think, to disappoint him in this, not
supplying the required gossamer grasp.

Very generously he later allowed me to come to Sherborne
for weekends only, when Carolyn had taken up residence there
with Claudia and Cressida. Her motives for doing this were, I
suspect, somewhat mixed, and not totally unconnected with my
own previously expressed fascination with Gurdjieff. But more
of this later. As you see quite clearly, I run ahead of myself.

First I had the dreadful task of breaking the news of this
now serious affair to Carolyn. After the inevitable deceits, the
matter was somewhat taken out of my hands in New York on,
quite appropriately, the anniversary of the St Valentine's Day
Massacre.

I had been invited by a bookstore with the highly felicitous
name of Murder Inc. to host a party in a local garage realistically
embellished to resemble the vaunted gangster slaughterhouse.

Almost forgetting this, I had run out of the apartment at the
last moment, leaving a love letter from Diane open on my
desk. There's no such thing as an accident. Unconsciously, if
that is what it was, I had done what I had dreaded – and needed
to do. My return to my own private slaughterhouse I need
hardly describe. Glacial misery will do, though tempered, I
suspect by a soupçon of precognition on my wife's part. Did

I want to leave her? Could I really leave our life, our home, our children?

We took an agonizing holiday in Antigua, seeded with long, circumlocutory and tortuous, as well as torturing, speeches. With my sudden and necessary interest in Gurdjieff and spiritual transformation not only as the self-excapulatory excuse for my betrayal but also as the currency of my communication, a fugue of joint supplicant memories became entwined with the inexorable evaded knowledge of parting. In a tired phrase, the holiday from hell. We returned to New York with nothing decided but everything effectively terminated.

I went to the West Coast to stay with my good friend Leo Rost. Carolyn, somewhat ill-advisedly, flew to England, heavily pregnant, and lost the baby – another girl, as I was roughly told, having flown from the West Coast, by an intern at the hospital who had in his own words 'disposed of it'. We had some days of mourning, though for some reason I never told her the sex of the dead child (but I later discovered she knew it anyway).

Divorce inexorably followed, though staved off by a number of half-hearted (that is, on my part) reconciliations. Little did I know what this shilly-shallying was doing to the children, only finding out much later from my eldest daughter Claudia, who told me that when she heard my car start up in the late evenings she somehow knew that I was gone again and after some time would cry herself to sleep. Emotional pressure or not, it left its mark, as did my craven act of leaving Cressida's birthday present on the steps of our Tregunter Road house without seeing her.

And so it was to the courts and the grotesque wrongness of it. It was surreal – a series of events happening to one, seemingly as if they were happening to someone else. I am glad to be able to jump ahead to today and report that most of that is now healed and Carolyn and I are the very best of friends, exchanging dinner and theatre dates on almost a fortnightly basis.

Anyway, after some time living at Diane's place, Scott's Farm in Wiltshire, she sold it and returned to Australia, mainly, I think, to spend some time with her aged parents, who were in their early nineties, before the inevitable happened. Sir Raphael Cilento was a merry, roguish man of formidable intellect, talents and achievements, who among other things had been head of the World Health Organisation.

Having followed Diane to Australia, I was lucky enough to meet him before his terminal decline started and he was to spend five virtually silent years with his eyes closed and his leg amputated to prevent gangrene, stubbornly fighting the Grim Reaper in a Catholic hospital outside Brisbane staffed by even grimmer nuns.

He would tease his almost as distinguished wife Phyllis, aka, Mother MD and Medical Mother of Australia on her popular radio programmes, by making provocatively spicy remarks under his breath, such as, 'It really doesn't matter who rubs a piece of skin against another's. After all, all cats are grey in the dark.'

'What's that, dear?' she would ask sharply.

'Nothing, dear,' he would reply placatingly. 'I was just reflecting on the ubiquity of love.'

He was a commanding and urbane man, exceedingly good company and a fountain of provocative if not outrageous opinion. I only once found him discombobulated. We were sitting alone and were talking about the Socratic arguments for the existence of the soul, when he suddenly said, 'You know, I have opened up at least 10,000 human beings and I have never found the soul!'

I laughed, and when he glowered I asked, 'Have you ever found a sense of humour?'

It was his turn to laugh, albeit ruefully, and to admit that his statement had been one of the silliest things he had ever said.

It was a generous admission, showing the nature of a great man, a state of being which of course was finally recognized by the state funeral he was accorded and that I had the honour to attend.

His wife, Phyllis, was also a formidable figure, presiding over a court of flattering and sycophantic servants in Glen Road, Brisbane. Born in Adelaide under the name of McGlew she was a widely respected person with great influence based as much as anything on the fact that she had apparently brought half the leading politicians of the time into the world.

She was a great champion of vitamins C and E, persisting in her advocacy even though the medical profession by and large refused for many years to recognize their efficacy. Nor did the press precisely recognize what she had said. On one occasion they credited her with the alarming and improbable statement that vitamin C could cause hallucinations, when what she had really said was that it could cause 'loose motions'. What this did for Mr Bayer and his company remains unknown.

She was also furiously outspoken, believing, as she put it, that she was 'too old to be struck off'. Once when I took her to dinner, she conducted the restaurateur around the entire buffet as it lay under blazing display lights, apostrophizing each dish in turn.

'This fish must have been lying here since the turn of the century.

'This soup curdled a full month ago.

'If you ate that ham tart, you would be in rictus inside the hour.

'In fact I believe that half my patients must dine here before they come and see me,' etc., etc.

In the middle of one such dinner tête-à-tête, she suddenly interrupted my flow of social prattle with a glacial stare and demanded abruptly, 'Just when exactly is it that you are going to marry my daughter?!'

There was no real counter to this, so the nuptials were duly announced. The event took place under a large flowering bauhinia tree in our garden at Karnak, which we had named after the Egyptian temple on the left bank of the Nile facing the Valley of the Kings which had been the City of Lights, with a population of 10,000 priests, and is now in altered circumstances no less luminous, being the subject in the season of daily son et lumière.

A marriage celebrant from the hideous town of Mareeba officiated the ceremony, which combined the needs of exped-ition (not alas for the usual reasons) and efficacy in the sense that it was non-denominational – just as well, in the circum-stances, as so to speak Son of Zion was bonding with the daughter of Mary Magdalene. Our best man turned out to be a dullard, pinch-hitting for a good friend, actor and latter-day film producer called Lance Reynolds, who failed to turn up to do the honours; the stand-in's name I have mercifully forgotten but his only known sobriquet was Poisoned Pig II. (Poisoned Pig I was a despicable New Age freeloader, one of many we knew at the time, whose name I've also mercifully forgotten.)

In the company of the errant Lance Reynolds, who was later

a producer of the ill-starred *The Case of the Oily Levantine* in London, I had chosen a delicious wedding hat for Diane from the window of Yves Saint Laurent in Beverly Hills. Her wedding dress was bought from the designers who had made Princess Diana's wedding dress. I can only imperfectly describe it as a symphonic see-through collage of white crêpe shot through with silver beads and seedpearls. In the clear sunshine, Diane looked magnificent, witnessed by a cloud of electric blue butterflies which swarmed round the bauhinia blossom, and by many local friends and innumerable Cilento relatives, led by the triumphant lady of the tribe from a wheelchair. The only mar on the day was that I couldn't wear my own favourite white suit. The fly-zip had been mashed into the material by the local dry-cleaner and was stuck immovably in the down position. It doesn't take much to provoke an Australian crowd to obscene ribaldry, and wearing those trousers would have been not so much asking for trouble as sitting up and begging for it.

A piece from Ib'n Arabi's *Fesus 'Al Hikam* was read surprisingly badly by Poisoned Pig II, considering he had been a pupil at the Sufi School, Beshara, presided over by Bulent Rauf, a sheikh and savant who had himself actually translated it from the Arabic.

Then we were off to a reception at our own restaurant, the Nautilus, in Port Douglas (of which more later). There I made a somewhat confused speech about the state of marriage being imaged by birds in cages envying the freedom of their feathered friends outside, and the latter envying the security of those inside. After some genial jeers, I was welcomed into the family by Diane's brother Carl, and we departed for our honeymoon on Lizard Island in a small single-engined plane, where, as previously stated, the omnipresent Morris West lay in wait for us.

Now we were man and wife, and I briefly recalled La Rochefoucauld's aphorism about marriage quoted earlier: 'No matter whom you marry, you will discover the next morning that you have married someone else.'

I'm glad to say that it was not so in my case. This is not to say that the transition was unremarkable, but that it was simply confirmative. This, thank God, was not completely unexpected.

13. Karnak – *Fitzcarraldo,* Eat Your Heart Out!

Life in tropical rainforest Australia was pleasant enough, though somewhat unreal, for we were after all living in what was virtually a tourist resort area, with its concomitant influx and efflux of people. In addition, I had absolutely nothing in common with the resident population, mostly Italian and Scottish immigrant cane farmers.

My wife's Italian background built a sort of bridge to the neighbours. The eccentric Scomazzones kept as a pet a cassowary, a kind of gigantic, savage, plumed emu that they called Eeny-Meeny, until one day it ripped up a horse and had to be disposed of. The Berrys, Rhonda and Ron, though not Italian, were our nearest neighbours and shared Diane's passion for growing things. She was a good, though somewhat drab musician, who finally found the courage to move south to be properly tutored. He stayed on to grow plantains (big bananas), which he showed to coachloads of people for money. I took the tour once and was astounded by what people pay to see. Watching plantains grow is something akin to watching paint dry, and the plantains covered with Rice Krispies and chocolate served in his little restaurant did absolutely nothing to ameliorate the misery.

Our first days at Karnak, christened by me the Great Green

Hell of Whyanbeel because of its razor-sharp guinea grass, most of which had to be dug up, and its prolific insect population, were spent painfully and painstakingly dismantling about 200 acres of barbed-wire fences that defended the various fields and pastures. The place had been a cattle station and more latterly a failed cane farm. After the construction of the theatre, and its long career as a spiritual centre and school whose students aided the myriad horticultural and building improvements, it became what the Melbourne newspaper *The Age* came to call 'a national treasure'.

Many people of all denominations thronged there from all over the world, its fame disseminated by among others Alan Whicker's TV programme *Whicker's World* and *Good Morning America*, and an exhaustive article in the *Sunday Times* colour supplement. Diane of course had achieved fame as an Australian ambassador and international filmstar in inter alia *The Agony and the Ecstasy* with Rex Harrison and Charlton Heston, *Hombre* with Paul Newman and *Tom Jones* with Albert Finney. She was also known for a number of extraordinary stage performances in, for example, Giradoux's *Tiger at the Gates* in London and on Broadway, *The Big Knife* with Sam Wanamaker and *Castles in Sweden*. This, as well as her tireless optimism and fierce energy, helped considerably.

Diane seemed to be able to turn her hand to everything, from propagating fruit trees, to milking goats, to mending broken pipes in the water intake from one of the two creeks that bounded our property.

The houses in Karnak grew like Topsy until there were four of them, all grandiosely named: the Palace, the Ritz, the Château and the Castle. We lived in the last one, which contains, as the real estate agents call it, a wealth of stained glass magnificently created by Diane's brother David, a study of local wood with a sixty-foot ceiling (because I mistook metres for feet), and a sitting-room, made again of wonderful local wood, with a television that cannot under any circumstances be induced to work.

These houses are divided by plantations of coffee, grapefruit, mandarin, jackfruit, paw-paw, passion fruit, sapotes and soursop, the last a sinister green spiky-skinned fruit with a forbidding white pulpy interior that made the most lethal cocktails imaginable at our restaurant, the Nautilus, in Port Douglas.

All of these trees were thickly covered with savagely biting green ants and vengeful paper wasps. They were watered, as were the houses, by the ingenious, if frail, intake system from the local creek which was almost as unreliable as our television set. Occasionally the lack of water would be compensated for by the visit of a cyclone. Even as I write one has inflicted dreadful damage on our magically landscaped home. The 200-mile-an-hour winds threw down over 100 fruit trees, transferring some of them to the living-rooms of the houses and crushing roofs and ripping our theatre roof off, apart from depositing many hundreds of tons of water.

Yes, we have a theatre in the grounds of our house! A 500-seater virtually uncovered auditorium with the best sight lines and acoustics in the world. This came about as a result of a careless speech of my own. For many years I could have cut my tongue out for it.

Diane, finding me in pensive mood, not to say downright bored, asked me what I missed most living in Australia.

'The theatre,' I replied.

'Then why don't we build one?' she asked insouciantly.

To my temporary chagrin, I answered, 'What a good idea!'

Millions of dollars and revilements later, it was completed and opened in August 1992 in the presence of Mr Goss, then Premier of Queensland, and I came to feel much happier about it. During the building of it we were hounded unmercifully by the local Douglas Shire Mossman Council, who put every obstacle they could devise in our way, even demanding bribes before they would pass the local roads as fit for vehicular travel. The inhabitants of Mossman suspected wrongly and jealously that we were being government-funded (As$100,000 were given later – a puny sum in the overall financial scenario). Locals spat at us and hurriedly crossed the road when we appeared in the town, as if they were suddenly confronted by Mephistopheles. A poisoned pig (not our best man) was placed in our driveway, poisoned pen letters were sent to our neighbours, and a poisonous attempt was made to frame me on an obscenity charge to prevent me from being able to hold a bar licence.

Notwithstanding all this, there was great joy in the construction of the theatre. The labours to build a theatre in the jungle in the film *Fitzcarraldo* pale into insignificance by comparison. A former Mayor of South Melbourne had devised for us a Euclidean method of raising the huge poles that underpinned the building. To our unbounded surprise, after much frenzied and to me unfollowable geometrical calculations, these rose magically from their prone positions on the ground to a perfect upright, and so in a necromantic manner inspired us to redouble our efforts to build our theatre in the rainforest.

In the absence of the local council but, as I have indicated, to state imprimatur, we opened to great enthusiasm with my own

Murderer supported by a ballet and other national acts. The play, entirely rewritten for the occasion, was directed by Diane and featured Australia's most prestigious Shakespearean actor, John Stanton, and, for one unscheduled performance only, our cat Calico. The former was on the whole dull and tiresome to work with, the latter was simply carnivorous – she intermittently ate one of the props, a rib of beef, attacking it with gusto every time the actor was on the higher level of the split set, out of her sight. This performance got the biggest laughs of the evening, as the unfortunate thespian continuously checked his flies and other vital parts of his costume and make-up in vain attempts to detect the source of the audience's merriment. The cat of course, being a theatre pussy, timed her assaults on the meat perfectly, listening to the dialogue, hearing his descending foot-steps and hiding when he came downstairs.

Though we have done a well-attended *Midsummer Night's Dream*, with a fine cast of seventy-nine, and a dazzling laser show, which was a kind of cosmic history lesson featuring myself as the voice of God, we have, alas, struggled for audiences. It's not so much that among the local population theatre is a dirty word as that they have never heard the word in the first place. Even the council's building inspector, who laid down a thousand or two harassing structural changes to be made in the building, displayed an astonishing disentitlement for the job.

'Are people going to be coming here at night time?' he asked forbiddingly, seeking a new reason for banning or changing what we had done.

'They mostly do go to the theatre at night,' I assured him. 'Why, are you surprised?'

'I wouldn't know,' he replied. 'I've never been in one before.'

At least he was better than his predecessor, who'd been committed to a lunatic asylum after his approved cyclone-proof structures in Darwin had been entirely blown away by Cyclone Tracy in the 1980s.

Now that we're up and running, an esteemed national concert venue after the recent visit of the – in contemporary parlance – bipolar, dysfunctional pianist David Helfgott (of *Shine* fame), we are still struggling for audiences. It may be the remoteness of the place, or the local phenomenon of no one needing to be told a story of any kind, I simply don't know – but either way it's their funeral! But perhaps I'm misjudging them.' Things have improved quite dramatically recently, with the latest play *The Thing in the Wheelchair* (May 2001), directed quite electrically by my wife, Diane, with enough spirited fun to take the curse off the grim storyline. Hailed by David Williamson, the doyen of Australian playwrights, as the most entertaining play he has seen in the country for as long as he could remember, and by a senior local newspaper critic as 'a cyclone of a thriller/ melodrama' this (to quote our media release) is the story of a Lady Macbeth of the suburbs – a pitiless, torturing, erotically fixated, murderous woman who indulges her fiendish fantasies, and not only 'screws her courage to the sticking point' as Lady Macbeth herself had, but goes far beyond it. Neither is she 'too full of the milk of human kindness to catch the nearest way'. If she delays it is only to indulge some fresh invention of diabolical cruelty. Battling her to save her son's life is a completely paralysed, defenceless old woman, wheelchair bound and speechless. In short, it is a melodrama in the somewhat forgotten tradition of Patricia Hamilton's *Rope and Gaslight* and Emlyn Williams' *Night Must Fall*, and has proved a real crowd pleaser, swelling our audiences to three or four times their normal size.

Nevertheless, I'm still inclined to agree with George B. Leonard in his *Education and Ecstasy* that 'our expectations of what this human animal can learn, can do, can be, remains remarkably low and timorous'.

14. The Nautilus, and Afterwards

Some little time before the theatre venture, we embarked on another enterprise of which we had even less experience. We bought a restaurant, one of the oldest in Australia – thirty years old – the Nautilus, in Port Douglas.

The beautiful old place, located up on a hill and somewhat celebrated, was owned by Max Bowden, a strange exile and claimed descendant of Harry Hotspur who had lived since the end of the Second World War on the same hill in something of a cloud of mystery. He never left the hill, was a keen gardener and employed relays of pretty girls whom he constantly advocated thrashing. His wife Diana, whom he had met in sinister circumstances in Bonn, was a mistress of the rum bottle, European languages, shell jewellery and flourless chocolate cake.

One evening they had arrived at our house for dinner and Max was looking particularly gloomy. Having completely failed to joke him out of it, I finally asked if there was anything I could do to help.

'No,' he repeated stubbornly, 'there is nothing to be done.'

I finally wormed it out of him. The bank, in its customary unfeeling way in the Antipodes, had foreclosed on him, and he needed a sizeable sum of money in a hurry.

I instantly proposed a loan, but he turned it down.

'I never take loans,' he said grandly. 'It's a matter of principle. "Neither a lender nor a borrower be",' he quoted sonorously, which in the circumstances I thought was not only pretty stupid but also patently untrue as he was already plainly in hock to the bank. The discussion continued in a desultory and semi-inebriated fashion until the wee small hours, when he suddenly said, 'You've always like the Nautilus restaurant, haven't you? Why don't you buy it, then?'

I agreed that it certainly seemed a way out of the impasse, and so it was that I became for As$150,000 the totally inexperienced owner of one of the most prestigious watering holes in Australia.

Sportingly, the next day he phoned up offering to allow me to renege on the deal as one 'having been struck in wine'. But it was my turn to refuse. After all, his bank was still pursuing foreclosure, and to tell the truth I was secretly rather intrigued by the thought of becoming a restaurateur, as was Diane, to whom I had casually observed earlier that day, 'By the way, we bought the Nautilus restaurant last night.'

She fell upon the place with her usual invention and appetite. Within a comparatively short time we were furnished with plate-glass tables (most of them, alas, almost immediately smashed by falling coconuts), which stood on a newly bricked terrace in the shape of a nautilus shell that we ourselves laid down. We were up and running with me at the entrance, greeting people with soursop cocktails held in dusky-red, sand-papered brickie's hands.

Getting customers proved surprisingly difficult at the time. (This was before the huge Mirage hotel put the town truly on the tourist map.) Things were looking fairly parlous until we thought of Sunday lunches!

The place, when we had customers that is, was tending to become somewhat cliquey, with the same punters bellying up to the bar and monopolizing it. Diane suggested using the chef's day off to introduce new blood, not only into our menu but also into the patrons. Thus every Sunday the nationality of the restaurant changed, with the food being matched by the appropriate decor, staff uniform and music. Pommie Day (Yorkshire pudding and a baron of beef especially imported from the south, since the heat tended to burn the fat off the local Droughtmaster beef cattle), with myself as chef, was succeeded by French Day, Greek Day, Polish Day, Italian Day, Czech Day, etc., etc. These were serviced by local immigrant chefs and supported by their coterie of friends, who would come and see how they made out, or of course failed to do so, as many of them secetly hoped. This was the secret ingredient which kept the pot boiling. Their fierce, talented and competitive endeavours were promoted by fairly eccentric radio commercials composed by myself and enacted by the hapless, impressed cook-for-the-week. They would sit, stars for the day, terrified of the alien studio and their battle with the microphone and the clock. Thirty seconds did not mean thirty-one seconds, and all words – although heavily accented – had to be clearly enunciated and dramatized.

I remember an unfortunate Frenchman called Marcel struggling helplessly with a piece of tripe I had written for him. It described the 'crack of the suicide's gun' on the beach near the casino at Le Touquet, signifying the end of the life of a poor ruined punter who would never have killed himself had he known about the culinary delights of the Nautilus, and how cheap they were.

But all was not quite plain sailing. We were harassed by an officious copper, who plied his invidious profession under the sobriquet of Dirty Dave. His aim was to catch us out evading Queensland's antiquated licensing laws. He would peer from behind palm trees, crouch behind cacti, linger behind lilies, hide behind hybrids and lurk behind lattices, seeking to surprise us selling liquor out of hours.

His actions finally forced me to obtain a copy of the licensing laws, in which I discovered that on Sundays all drinks had to be paid for before two o'clock. But it didn't say they couldn't be served later on! It was the work of a moment to instruct our stalwart topers that each of them had to place at least fifty dollars in a top hat behind the bar before two o'clock. When that was used up, they could drink no more. When Dirty Dave finally pounced triumphantly on our merry throng one Sunday at 2.15 p.m., he was to be confounded by the information that all drinks had been paid for before 2 p.m., and were therefore entirely legal. I think it just about broke his heart, and if it didn't, his colleagues at the police station finally completed the job by stitching him up with a crock of cannabis planted in his locker. At any rate he left the area and we had no more trouble.

Year has followed year, making for round about two decades at Karnak, the years marked by the annual Wet, which can come at any time between Christmas and March and lasts for up to six weeks, drumming incessantly on the tin roofs like machine-gun fire on the Somme, prohibiting conversation, covering our clothes with mould (I once searched lengthily but vainly for a new brown flannel suit, only finally to discover it –

turned completely green), gumming pages of books together, washing away vital bridges, known footpaths, and telephone wires, and bringing in train its inevitable depression. May, June and July are cane-burning months, the sugar content being increased by the fire's intensity, and the beauty of the rainforest countryside dramatically heightened by the roar of the conflagrations, and the rolling black clouds of smoke and flame which briefly obscure the jungle mountains but highlight the snakes and bandicoots fleeing for their lives. The Crushing starts in June and ends when it's done. In November, the poinciana, jacaranda, bougainvillaea and other tropic plants bloom riotously, and the mangoes ripen and plummet from the trees, ten pounds the piece in Fortnum and Mason, there for taking on the Queensland highways. Finally there are the roasting Yuletides, featuring endless taped carols in the supermarkets and ludicrously inappropriately garbed Father Christmases, sweating away inside heavy red serge uniforms and cotton-wool beards as they bring cheer to the scalding high streets and vast sandy beaches.

I would still be there full-time if only the mental stimulation had equalled the fierce energy and probing skills of the alternating 'footie' and cricket that also marked the seasons of the year.

But alas, it was not to be. Return to England became inevitable, at least for longer periods of the year. Once again, I had perhaps expected too much of my new way of life.

15. Agatha Christie, and Other Cinematic Reflections

But I run ahead of myself, yet again. At the time of writing it is the spring of 2000, reminding me in its bounteous blossoming of another English advantage – the seasons; tropical Australia really doesn't have them. Yet I can't believe that I have turned my back on everything there. The arctic beer and the towel-covered counters; the terrible T-shirts and the thongs; the rough camaraderie ('Sport', 'Blue', 'Mite') and the putrid pavs (Pavlovas made with cream and meringue); my Great Dane/dingo Max and his new child bride Molly, who later was to have eight enchanting, healthy puppies; my lofty, book-lined study with its quilla shelves, giant carved-wood manta ray, vast seminal Arthur Boyd painting and stained-glass windows; and even the truly saddening desolation of the isolation.

All this is probably a monstrous piece of sentimentality. When I was living there full-time I was often pleased to escape to work, on the whole not tremendously successfully, in an even more isolated desert – Hollywood. I laboured for most of the Majors, for Fox and for Warners, and Universal, and Paramount, and MGM, but not, as the lawyers would say in another connection, with full and effective penetration. It may have been my own arrogance, intemperance or continual feeling of derision that prevented me from bringing more of these endless endeavours to climax.

The limitless timidity of the producers was their chief feature. Never do anything that hasn't been done successfully a trillion times before, which naturally means financially successfully rather than creatively: that was the cornerstone of their cogitations. This saved them from thinking or using their imaginations, since the correct criteria were already firmly in place for judging all projects. What naturally resulted was a lifeless wasteland of overworked ideas, presided over by grotesquely rich, conformist tyrants, made pathologically neurotic by the lunatic, wasteful overspending of a fundamentally ignorant industry.

That I approached each project with dedicated hope and genuine excitement was I suppose to my credit, as was also to have those feelings crushed seriatim, and still be possessing them today with regard to any new creative venture.

Or, of course, it may be an act of the purest folly. Henry Miller thought so. In *The Cosmological Eye* he wrote: 'Hope is a bad thing. It means that you are not what you want to be. It means that part of you is dead, if not all of you. It means that you entertain illusions. It's a sort of spiritual clap I should say.'

Nevertheless, I should say that hope is still a quintessential ingredient of all endeavour. Even the gloomiest of pessimists, Franz Kafka, notes in his *Diaries*: 'If I were another person observing myself in the course of my life, I should be compelled to say that it must all end unavailingly, be consumed in incessant doubt, creative only in its self-torment. But as an interested party I go on hoping.'

I have already noted some of the Hollywood endeavours: *Jekyll and Hyde*, *Bela Lugosi*, *Sting II*, and others too numerous and too painful to recall. Even the most fruitful of them, *Frenzy*, was essentially an English film, shot in London by an English director, so it may be in the end a simple matter of nationality, horses for courses. Perhaps I was never destined to be a Hollywood writer; neither were Fitzgerald, or Huxley, or Chandler, or a host of others who fell substantially at the same fence. At home, though, we made a better fist of things cinematically.

Sleuth was followed by *The Wicker Man*, with its most curiously chequered history. I've already given an account of the making of this film, and even though it has acquired cult status, which demands its every move be lovingly and endlessly recalled, I fancy that in this narrative that single telling will suffice.

More than a quarter of century later the film is still being celebrated by the fanzines, a reissued music track on CD and innumerable television showings. And lately I have, by popular demand you might also say, been induced to write a follow-up. Abhorring sequential Roman numerals in film titles, I gave this one the name of *The Loathsome Lambton Worm*, but I suspect it will still end up as *Wicker Man II*.

Being such an anti-establishment pagan figure, it was not surprising that *The Wicker Man* was not commanded to appear before the Defender of the Faith at a Royal Command Film Performance, which was the distinguished fate of two of my other British films, subsequently made for EMI – Agatha Christie's *Death on the Nile* and *Evil Under the Sun*.

Having offered a certain amount of anonymous assistance to Sidney Lumet in preparing *Murder on the Orient Express*, I was rewarded by a request of the producers, Lord Brabourne and Richard Goodwin, in view of the success of the picture, to take on the Poirot series. This meant immuring myself in my study with all of the Poirot books piled up on the floor with a view to selecting follow-ups. I could get no assistance from the Dame herself, as unfortunately she was no longer with us.

Death on the Nile seemed to offer the most spectacular location of them all, and it was to be followed by *Evil Under the Sun*, which had a not too dissimilar plot but much wickeder over-tones (even Dame Agatha herself was worried that it might have been copycatted in real life!).

After the success of *Orient Express*, the decision to cram the films with stars was continued, and *Nile* led off with Bette Davis, Maggie Smith, David Niven, Angela Lansbury, Mia Farrow, Lois Chiles, Jack Warden, Jane Birkin, Edward Kennedy and Simon MacCorkindale, with Peter Ustinov replacing Albert Finney as Poirot. I like to think that change was for the better, as in *Orient Express* I found Poirot's dead-bat hair-do ludicrous, and his accent impenetrable.

The script had to be fairly grossly exaggerated, not to say sent up, since the original, like all the Christie novels, was very flatly written. It was always something of a mystery to me that the most revolutionary storyteller of our times was certainly the most pedestrian stylist.

Perhaps it had to be so. The whole 'I'll show you a mystery' is all very well, but if only a few can 'behold' it – by which I mean understand it – then it's all a bit of a waste of time. I also know that the phrase the 'most revolutionary storyteller of our times' is a bit contentious, but I believe it. Agatha Christie unquestionably invented the detective story – well, not perhaps unquestionably, since claims have been made in support of Wilkie Collins's *The Moonstone*. Even though T. S. Eliot called it 'the first, the longest and the best detective story', in my opinion it is only the longest and certainly not the best; after all, Sergeant Cuff failed to solve the mystery and retired to grow roses! Émile Gaborieau has his champions, in very strong support of which are *L'Affaire Lerouge*, as early as 1866, and *The Mystery of Orcival* (1867), and his archetypal detective, Monsieur Lecoq. And of course there are Edgar Allen Poe and Conan Doyle too, but I don't really think that 'The Murders in the Rue Morgue' quite does the trick, except in respect of its least likely simian murderer, and Holmes's genius shone only in the short stories. The long novels, even *The Hound of the Baskervilles*, are pretty tedious and detectivally bereft. No, Christie stands paramount. Despite the endlessly ingenious shifts of time and space with which she succeeded in bamboozling us for years, she basically only had three or four plots (vide *Death on the Nile* and *Evil Under the Sun*, wherein much the same shift of time and space exists). She virtually invented the completely original device of the 'least likely' suspect and though today the overuse of it in her oeuvre means that her murderers are quite easy to spot (just pick the one who couldn't possibly have done it), we must remember that it is half a century later.

Just as Conan Doyle hated Holmes, Christie loathed her hero, Poirot − 'that bloody little Belgian' she came to call him. It is not recorded what Doyle called Holmes, but the affair of the Reichenbach Falls clearly shows his state of mind when he tried to knock off the supercilious old fellow.

Death on the Nile was a pleasant enough shoot, interspersed with bouts of gastoenteritis and curious attempts by myself to enter my hotel bedroom other than by way of its permanently keyless door. I used instead a window via a most perilous ladder.

(My taxi cab was pursued by the manager waving the key as I left on the last day.) Further episodic occurrences were the almost daily bouts of violent ill humour from John Guillermin, the film's director. It was always a keen pleasure back in London to watch rushes and hear him dancing with rage on his cap, which he would have thrown to the floor. On one occasion, however, this intemperance was entirely justified.

This occurred in Pinewood Studios towards the end of the shoot during the endless dénouement that Christie fans demand – a lengthy wrap-up, packed with red herrings, while the great H. P. enlightens us as to what has really been going on and why wholly apparently disassociated events and objects are all linked in a diabolical pattern which reveals whodunnit. He doesn't ever explain why, by the time the 'leetle cells gris' grind into action, most of his clients have already been murdered, but that would be asking too much, since if they hadn't been he would have had very little to do.

On this particular occasion, Peter Ustinov as Poirot had uttered the classic introductory words to such a scene – 'You may all be wondering why I have asked you here tonight' or something equivalent – then proceeded to embark on a lengthy unravelling of the plot in the presence of the stellar suspects – Bette Davis, Maggie Smith, Mia Farrow, Jane Birkin, Angela Lansbury, James Mason, Jack Warden, Edward Kennedy and Simon MacCorkindale, all of whom were grouped more or less dumbly around the walls of the grand salon. They were mostly silent because Poirot had an awful lot to explain, and I didn't want any interruptions to the complex narrative except, of course, for the usual hysterical denials of the finally accused murderer.

Bette Davis was having none of this. She wanted some lines. She hadn't in her quaint argot, 'been hired to be a goddamned dummy'. I explained the situation, pointing out to her that no one else had any lines either, but it cut little ice. Exasperated at her continuing demands, I said to her, 'You're not going to have any more lines, Bette. Those you've had already you've either précised, paraphrased, or entirely forgotten.'

'Bastard,' she snarled in her familiar, lovable manner and the battle lines were drawn.

Shooting started, and on each take the camera operator reported a flash on his track-in. A rehearsal would be ordered and invariably it would be clean. In the next take, however, the flash would equally invariably appear. During the next three hours, take ten became take twenty, twenty became thirty, and so on, until we reached take fifty with the irascible Guillermin apostrophizing the luckless operator, who had no ready explanation of why he couldn't perfect matters in the allotted rehearsal time.

Having finished my work and with nothing much to do, I was strolling about, still fairly dubious of Miss Davis, and it was at this point that I finally detected the source of the trouble. Bette had concealed a mirrored compact in her muff and on every take would withdraw and flash it with the express intention of drawing attention to herself. It was unbelievable. Here was a world star, with over 100 movies to her credit, prepared to sabotage at Lord knows what cost, at least half a day's work with a dozen or so other world stars just to satisfy her bloated ego because she hadn't got any lines.

I held out my hand for the compact, saying, 'Your make-up is just perfect, Bette,' reflecting as I did so that this quality is probably what it takes to become a great movie star – and remain one for half a century.

Evil Under the Sun was a somewhat more light-hearted affair, with its extravagant thirties costumes, created by Anthony Powell, and its Cole Porter score, wonderfully tailored by the poor man's Tommy Beecham, John Lanchberry. The cast was again multi-stellar. Peter Ustinov, David Niven, Maggie Smith and Jane Birkin were joined by James Mason, Diana Rigg, Colin Blakely, Roddy McDowell and Nicholas Clay.

It didn't quite do the same business as *Nile* at the outset, but I understand that it is catching up, and it is still my favourite. At any rate it certainly far outstrips the perfectly dreadful Christie film *Appointment With Death*, which I part-wrote. It was bought up from EMI's catalogue by the self-approbatory and wholly tasteless Michael Winner, who made every mistake he could, including removing the film from its original enchanted setting of Petra and rewriting a lot of the picture himself. John Gielgud told me that it was the most leaden script he had ever read and I must say that I agreed with him. As I'm sure would have Euan Ferguson, who said of Winner in the *Observer* recently on another matter, 'He aims low and misses.'

One of the many faults of the film business is that it makes unsolicited bedfellows out of everybody: you simply buy a property from a defunct film company and make it. Taking your name off it is far too expensive, in this case $50,000. If you can't afford it, you must hope that the whole mess will shortly go away almost unnoticed, which mercifully is what came to pass.

But this might be simply to confirm Allen Tate in his poem 'To The Lacedemonians': 'Men expect too much; do too little'.

16. *Forbush and the Penguins*

My very first film had been a romantic comedy set mostly in the Antarctic, with John Hurt and a couple of leading ladies – the first, Susan Fleetwood, having been peremptorily replaced at the rough cut stage by Hayley Mills – and a cast of thousands – of penguins that is. *Forbush and the Penguins* was also, unfortunately, a decade or so before its time, being concerned with man's relationship with his environment: it climaxes with Hurt interfering with the natural order of things by trying to sort out the skuas with a home-made Roman ballista as a punishment for preying on penguin chicks. This of course is an abysmal failure, forcing him to realize that that particular war is as old as time, and that in spite of their depredations a satisfactory proportion of the chicks survive every year, while the others are simply hostages to natural fortune.

It was produced by Bryan Forbes and chiefly financed by the National Film Finance Corporation as well as EMI and British Lion in shares believed equal to the NFFC's, which as Alexander Walker pointed out at the time was a departure from the traditional trade practices, under which the principal distributors do not normally finance each other's films. He also pointed out the film ran into difficulties that might have furnished material for an Ealing comedy. The absolutely marvellous penguin/skua footage shot by the Swedish director and cameraman Arne Suckersdorff, who had spent weeks of an Antarctic winter alone to get it, either wouldn't fit with the human sequences of Al Viola (the film's American director) or was almost entirely ignored by him. It took Roy Boulting to force a belated screening of it. It was Viola's first feature film, and from time to time his inexperience manifested itself in risible gaffes. In one set of rushes that I saw, he printed a stage direction as dialogue ('Blah . . . Blah . . . Blah! firmly shoots a starched cuff!').

In the event Roy Boulting galloped to the rescue and shot some new material with his wife Hayley Mills, which in my opinion did little to help the film. But at least he knew the difference between dialogue and stage directions, and the re-working put the film's release from its completion at the beginning of 1971 back to the end. Unfortunately the box office receipts were less than brilliant and in no way rewarded the arduous conditions of the location shoot in the Antarctic. Everyone had lived in Shackleton's hut built at the turn of the century and outside of which the conditions were scarcely easier because of the sudden descent of blizzards, so blinding that people had to rope themselves to homebase when taking a walk to be certain of finding their way back.

A release a decade or so later would have made all the difference. My younger daughter Cressida likes it the most out of my cinematic endeavours, as do many of her young friends, proving that it's not always wise to be avant-garde.

Still, I had broken my duck, and Bryan Forbes's endless recounting of his perturbed dreams of sleeping with Her Majesty the Queen were alone worth the price of admission to the exalted world of EMI.

Also, I think I had broken the duck of ecology-conscious films (it was the first of the trend of movies concerned with the balance of nature), though now when I hear the buzz words 'environment' and 'ecology' and 'organic' tagged on to anything and everything remotely connected to the natural order of things I rather wish I hadn't bothered. Mea culpas for the ozone holes, and missing hedgerows, and barren seas, and silent springs, and the twisted limbs of our children, and our woolly, poisoned brains, and the infertile deserts of the world, and so forth: they grow fantastically tedious.

But there are fewer mea culpas for our more dubious expectancies – the wonder drugs, the telecommunication marvels, the blind belief in the scientists who will sort out our brave new world!

As Charles Sanders Pierce reminds us in his *Collected Papers*, 'It is a common observation that those who dwell continually upon their expectations are apt to become oblivious to the requirements of their actual situation.'

17. *The Case of the Oily Levantine* and *This Savage Parade* and *Widow's Weeds*

The Case of the Oily Levantine (or *Whodunnit* as it was known in the States) was produced by two Antipodeans – Lance Reynolds and Fred Bestall – and it did not enjoy the greatest good fortune in the West End, where it played the almost unplayable Her Majesty's Theatre. Built by Beerbohm Tree, it's more suited to musicals, with their bigger sounds; the huge orchestra pit fatally separates the stage from the auditorium and the stalls and the circle are almost equally totally divided – a laugh takes about ten minutes to travel from the one to the other. The show was directed by Patrick Dromgoole, the real discoverer of Joe Orton (he was the first to direct *Entertaining Mr Sloane*) and later managing director of Harlech Television. We had a super cast of, amongst others, Hywel Bennett, Adrian Costa, Anna Quayle, Gwen Nelson, Wolfe Morris and William Squire, as well as the fine stage designer Hayden Griffin.

Unfortunately Patrick shot himself in the foot by casting Hywel in two roles, those of the murdered man and the inspector investigating the murder, on the grounds that we needed a big star, which actually he wasn't. I compounded the *bêtise* by going along with it. After *Sleuth* the audience was expecting a splendid trick of some kind, which had never in fact been contemplated. They thought this odd bit of casting was the ploy. Further, our horrendous first night scarcely got us off to a great start. At least 300 seats in prominent positions were empty, which was puzzling, as we had been assured that there wasn't a seat left in the house.

Although I had done my previous stage works with Michael White, I hadn't sold this play to him, and he had been heard to say that he would like to run my new producers out of town. For a while I suspected him of a dastardly but simple trick that he was well placed to execute – viz., that of buying up the tickets so that the theatre seemed full, but then flushing them down the loo. Suspicion was deepened when investigation of relevant cheques in the box office seemed to indicate a company similarly named to one of Michael's, but upon confrontation he swore he had not done it and would never have been capable of doing so. I believed him and normal relations were restored. It turned out that some parties in our producing company had tried to scalp their own first night and had been caught with the tickets, having been unable to sell them. Unfortunately the faint reception from the depleted house badly threw our cast, who on tour had grown used to lots of laughs and other positive reactions. We sank slowly without trace.

On Broadway we did much better. Though we had a churlish reception from the almost totally humourless Frank Rich in the *New York Times*, we recovered after a rave from John Simon in *New York Magazine* ('a steamer trunk full of ideas'). Clive Barnes went back on his first dismissive notice, after the rapid opening and closing of a play called *Moosehead Murders*, with a fine notice including the notable phrase 'compared with *Moosehead Murders, Whodunnit* is *Hamlet!*'

In the event we ran six months on Broadway at the Biltmore, a considerable feat of longevity for the time. At least thirty other productions opened and closed during this run. This was all unlooked to. A bad *Times* review is almost always a killer. Furthermore, the out-of-town try-out in Boston had been dire. The director, Michael Kahn, had entirely lost his nerve and the star, Jack Weston, had been completely incompetent (he didn't put the book down until the dress rehearsal, and not really even then). We were only saved by the gallant George Hearne, who replaced him and who opened after only about ten days' rehearsal and endless rewrites, in which I was considerably aided by my wife Diane.

Incidentally a curious event that took place during the first try-out of this play at the Yvonne Arnaud Theatre, Guildford, with George Cole in the lead, enabled me to give my version of the famed Pirandello cigarette, which I liked to think was as good as the original. This is a device that at a stroke changes the whole nature of a play, its time structure or character delineation, and thus its plot. It may only be a small detail, but its effect is devastating. For example, in Pirandello's *Henry IV* the audience believes for most of the first act that it is witnessing a medieval drama centring on a crazy old king and his courtiers. At the end of the act he lights a cigarette, and this simple gesture immediately repositions this play in the twentieth century – we come to realize that the whole thing is a game played by a man pretending to be mad.

In *The Case of the Oily Levantine*, a spoof of the Agatha

Christie country house party stories, all the participating guests turn out to be actors paid to play the roles of the stock Christie characters — ingénue, military man, cad, florid foreigner, old maid, etc., etc. One night George Cole's moustache fell off, deeply humiliating him as he struggled vainly to replace it as the rest of the cast stood around giggling. I realized, of course, what a splendid Pirandello cigarette it was — if it had only happened to the right character — i.e., one of the suspects and not the inspector who comes to investigate the murder played by George. All evening we are a step ahead of the audience, teasing them with complicated voice-over clues to the murder's identity and promising momentary revelations; now an actor's moustache falls off and the rest of the cast 'corpse' at his embarrassment. For the first time the audience thinks that it is ahead of us. Let them have their fill of laughing, I thought, then let the inspector say to the moustacheless man, 'And does the rest come off too?' — he is receiving the same information as the audience. He and his fellow guests are all actors! The laughter in the audience dies. It's been booby-trapped again, and the play has totally changed direction!

This Savage Parade was a play about the capture of Eichmann by the Israelis. It had a twisty, whodunnit-like, courtroom format, which excited the wrath of Bernard Levin at its first presentation in Crewe, who really had no right to be there in his professional capacity of London theatre critic in the first place. He said that I had used the death of six million Jews merely to tell a detective story, and that this was impermissible.

To this day I don't see why. Frankly, I thought I had done a hell of a lot more, including making the point that the Jews and the Nazis were to some extent identical. For the Chosen People, read Herrenvolk; both claim to have the durability of 1,000 years of longevity, etc., etc., and the one *needs* the persecution of the other eventually to concentrate its power after the diaspora into the state of Israel. 'For the Jews can only exist in adversity,' the villain says in the play. 'Persecute them, hound them, single them out for attack and all their generosity and inseparability comes flooding up out of them. They become a race again.'

This was never going to be a widely popular view with either Jews or Gentiles. The former were too used to a misty-eyed view of themselves as eternal victims, and the latter were simply ashamed of the Holocaust. We did get a tremendously emotional response, though, from the packed little houses at the enterprising Dan Crawford's King's Head in Islington, a remarkably persuasive pub venue. We would have gone much farther with it had it not been unfortunately trashed by the uncomprehending John Peters in the *Sunday Times*, whom I felt completely missed the point. Alternatively he may just unluckily have been present the night that Alfred Marks completely ruined the play by crossing downstage and throwing the elegiac Garfield Morgan off balance by treading on his toes in the middle of his climactic aria – a retired comic performs a pratfall? Between Peters and Marks, it's enough to make one expectorate!

Neither had ever really understood the play, and personified André Gaudin's observation that 'the quality of our expectations determines the quality of our action'.

The Case of the Oily Levantine was not truly alternatively titled as was *Widow's Weeds* or *For Years I Couldn't Wear My Black*. It was changed to accommodate a country that we thought might be seriously wrong-footed into thinking that the play was about Texas crude; after all, the perhaps apocryphal story has it that at one time the name of *The Rake's Progress* was changed to *The First Gentleman* on the grounds that people might think it was a gardening film! On the other hand, *For Years I Couldn't Wear My Black* was a genuine case of ambivalence. In Brisbane, Australia, where it was well directed by an impish, semi-anaesthetized leprechaun called Joe McCallum, we ended up with both titles on the marquee, and I'm glad to say did well with both. In England, where we played thirty-six dates around the country, breaking the house record in thirty-one of them with a stellar mainly TV cast, including Susan Hanson, Christopher Strauli, Shaun Curry, Gian Sammaco, Adrian Mills and Lisa Geoghan, we kept it solely to *Widow's Weeds*, so the jury is still out about which is the better marquee name. Unfortunately, because of the pantomime season our package fell apart and we couldn't bring it in. In Poland, whence I was sent a television version, the name is naturally indecipherable, as is mostly the plot.

This, I suppose, is something that those familiar with Polish jokes would have expected.

18. Ealing Studios

Sometime in, I think, late 1996, I was asked by the art director David Bill, who then headed up Ealing Studios, to become its head of creative development. Rather unwisely, as it turned out, I accepted, and was asked to front for it to the national press. During the following year I made many vainglorious statements, receiving thousands of supportive letters in return from people all over the country. I also read many hundreds of scripts from hopeful screenwriters, both they and I being under the ludicrously mistaken impression that Ealing had the remotest intention of making any of them.

Little did I or they realize that the studio was being run by a wayward, daydreaming drunk who imagined that he could do so from a garden in Gloucestershire, holding a wicker trug containing a mobile phone and a couple of bottles of vodka.

Despite the fact that my contract was never honoured, I worked hard and in good faith for them and make no apology for reproducing here my inaugural statement of policy to the media.

From time to time, it is necessary to reassert greatness.
Individual, idiosyncratic, nonconformist, humble,
necessary greatness, and that is precisely what Michael

Balcon, the paternalist, bespectacled, black-suited
Brumagen, did during his twenty-odd-year reign as
production chief of Ealing Studios from 1938 to 1959.
'The comedies were,' he once said, 'if you like, a mild
protest – but a protest about nothing more sinister than
the regimentation of the times after a period of war. I
think we were going through a mildly euphoric period
then – believing in ourselves and having some sense of –
yes it sounds awful – national pride. And if I were to
think and think I couldn't give you a deeper analysis.' No
man of course had more national pride than 'Mick'
Balcon. Wherever he worked, there lay the heart of
British films, and a British film according to his description
was one that 'projected Britain and the British character'.
'I want to make comedies about ordinary people with a
stray eccentric among them,' he said later. 'Films about
daydreamers, mild anarchists, little men who long to kick
the boss in the teeth.' Well, in my newly created role of
head of creative development at Ealing Studios, so do I.
But what exactly are these so-called Ealing comedies?
Why did they become so legendary, and is there a place
for a new generation of them today?

There are many who stridently affirm that under no
circumstances should we seek to return to our safe, timid,
insular, time warp mentality – to jokey, unimportant little
British films with no international appeal. Ealing comedies
will clearly head the list of these offenders.

But it must not be forgotten that these were the
pictures of sanity.

Then does this mean a steady diet of comedies? Not by

any means. It is now often forgotten that for every *Titfield Thunderbolt* there was a *Blue Lamp* or *It Always Rains on Sunday*, or for a *Hue and Cry* a *Nicholas Nickleby* or *Pink String and Sealing Wax*. For every *Lavender Hill Mob* there was a *Cruel Sea* or *Dead of Night*.

No, a balanced mix is the answer, as the Man in the Black Suit put it, as befits the national character: 'Fiction films which portray contemporary life in Britain in different sections of our society; films with an outdoor background of the British scene, screen adaptations of literary classics, films reflecting the aspirations not of governments or parties but of individuals.'

And again: 'We shall become international by being national.'

Is this pie in the sky? Jingoistic illusion? Chauvinist claptrap? The British film industry has done it before and can do it again. There must be no surrender to the mindless, debauching, gruntingly abysmal world of the American supermovies. We will fight them in the studios and in the post-production offices and in the movie houses.

And how are we going to do all this, do I hear you cry? Well, some things never change. And shoestrings are perennially with us. As before, so now. As Balcon himself said, 'In the absence of money, we'll have to make do with talent.'

And what kind of talent should that be? A talent first of all to write, and then to read – particularly the latter, for good readers are as rare as hen's teeth. Reading a screenplay is as complex a process as reading an X-ray or symphonic score. I once met a reader in the boardroom of one of the US majors who was dyslexic, a handicap which became only too glaringly apparent when he came to read *aloud* a speech of mine in a script which he claimed 'didn't work'. The Lord's Prayer would not have worked in the mouth of someone whose larynx froze on words even of one syllable.

Again, and again, I have noticed in Hollywood a quite appalling reluctance to read in the right way (or, for that matter, to read at all). Right way, of course, is to suspend *disbelief* as we try to do in the theatre. One producer I knew so identified with the lead character that he used to refer to him as 'I' continually – 'I would never do that' or 'I'm incapable of such thoughts or actions'. Useless to point out that the man in the script was a totally fictional character, completely different from himself. As a result the script discussions invariably broke down on page three, where the first seriously impersonal confrontational business took place. A further quotation from the former master of Ealing comes to mind: 'A film producer is only as good as the sum total of the quality of the colleagues with whom he works, and in this respect, I have been uniquely fortunate.' Little did I know at the time that I had not been so fortunate, alas.

E. V. Lucas believed that in England it is a very dangerous handicap to have a sense of humour. We at Ealing are going to have to confront that danger and appeal to the purity and gentleness and unbreakableness of the common people that so attracted D. H. Lawrence.

We are going to make English films again in the full

and complacent belief that the English possess too many agreeable traits to permit them to be as much disliked as they think and hope they are.

Robert Speight in *An Unbroken Heart* concluded: 'That is why I love England. It is so little, and so full, and so old.' And so is Ealing Studios. Now once again our doors are open to do it all over again and this time to a new society, which is perhaps more deeply sectioned by the presence in its midst of numerous immigrant nationalities. What they will have to share, however, is an all-embracing national sense of humour, which is after all the true champion of our civil liberties.

We must be prepared to be not only oversensitized minorities but the butt of ethnic lampoon occasionally should it be necessary. *The Man in the White Suit* could become *The Man in the White Dhoti*, or *Passport to Pimlico*, *Passport to the Fulham Souk*.

It wasn't to last however. It went broke very quickly and I didn't get paid, nor, more importantly, did I make a film there. I had also been induced to disappoint thousands of people in the country who had sincerely hoped for better things. As far as I was concerned, David Bill escaped whipping. At his urgent beseeching, I never sued him, and for all I know he still lives in vainglorious, isolated splendour in Gloucestershire.

Or perhaps I should have seen it all coming and expected it.

19. Music

My taste in music runs mostly to the classical, fuelled in the early days by my mother taking me to the Hallé Orchestra, then conducted by the great Barbirolli and Sir Henry Wood, and latterly by the London orchestras under Flash Harry, a.k.a. Sir Malcolm Sargent, and Sir Thomas Beecham. I remember the latter giving a concert in Margate when he was to play the Shostakovich Tenth Symphony. He turned to us and said: 'The parts of the symphony have not arrived, which is probably just as well as I don't suppose any of you would have been able to understand it. So in its place I'm going to play something that you *will* be able to understand.' And he turned round and played us the national anthem. Abrupt and rude, certainly, but he made amends by suddenly returning to the podium and giving the stunned audience a highly spirited rendition of Chabrier's *España*.

Among other eccentric or unusual concerts, I recall the pianist Pachmann handing round to members of the audience the scores he was performing for them to see how difficult they were to play, and a hair-raising Rubinstein concert at the Brighton Pavilion Dome when we ourselves had *Murderer* at the Theatre Royal. The fact that the two buildings were connected allowed our show's director, Clifford Williams, and me to secure last-minute seats on the platform in the hall.

As we sat there I happened to notice a man further down the line of spindly gold chairs behaving in a rather excitable fashion. The first half of the concert had come to an end and Rubinstein was taking his bow when the man suddenly ran forward and seized him by the hand from behind, lifting his arm high above his head. Apparently, he had just wanted to make a speech welcoming the great pianist to Brighton, but all he succeeded in achieving was making Rubinstein apprehensive about the frailty of his eighty-year-old hands as well as giving him a very severe shock, scared as he was about an assassination, as are many public performers. We carried him back to his dressing-room in a syncope, and not surprisingly he declined to come out and perform the second part of the concert.

My last time on a concert platform was at Vladimir Horowitz's triumphal return to London after thirty years, with tickets secured for me by my daughter Claudia, who had queued all night outside the Festival Hall. A gorgeous present, and fortunately he was able to complete the concert without any perturbed attempts at welcome to the city from which he had absented himself for so long.

On that occasion, after a douce, unshowy first half of children's pieces (some Schumann – 'Kindersgenen'), he recognized me from a previous occasion and said, 'You've had the pianissimos. I assure you things will change in the second half.' He was referring to a meeting that had taken place at least twenty years before at the country house of Morty Gottlieb in Connecticut. Horowitz, who was a neighbour, had come visiting and insisted that we went for a walk together. I found this absolutely terrifying, as he was my idol. Alongside the great man, I suddenly found myself tongue-tied, at the dead of night, walking round a frozen pond with turtles hibernating in its middle.

I remember slipping off his fur gloves to feel his fingers, which were as hard as iron. (Only years later did I discover he was homosexual, but he made no play in this direction.) Haltingly, I spoke of my admiration for him.

'But what do you admire most about my playing?' he asked.

'The speed, the drama,' I replied. 'But I must admit I sometimes miss the more reflective pianissimos,' I added haltingly.

'My pianissimos are astonishing,' he acclaimed. 'And my dynamics are world-famous. But surely you wouldn't want an entire concert of reflective pianissimos?' he asked slyly.

'Of course not, that's not exactly what I meant,' I floundered.

'Never mind that,' he said impatiently. 'Who do you think I play worst?'

I tried to avoid answering but he was insistent, so finally I blurted out, 'Beethoven.'

'You are probably correct,' he said, without a trace of resentment. 'But I will get him right. The trouble is that I find the sonatas too easy!'

This was such an astonishing statement that I changed the subject.

'Do you admire Rubinstein?' I asked.

'Of course,' he replied. 'But he doesn't earn anything like what I earn. Did you know that I take 95 per cent of the gross of all my concerts?'

'So you wouldn't rather be him, say as far as Beethoven is concerned, for example?'

'There are many pianists like Rubinstein,' he pronounced proudly. 'There is only one Horowitz!'

One had learned that the idol had feet of clay – arrogance. But if you listen to his recordings of, for example, the Liszt B Minor Sonata, or the 'Great Gate of Kiev' in 'Pictures at an Exhibition', or the A Flat Impromptu of Schubert, or the Tchaikovsky First Piano Concerto or the Rachmaninov Third, you will forgive him anything. He is right – there is only one Horowitz!

My first time on a concert platform was in 1940, again at the Brighton Pavilion Dome during their music festival – as a performer! I played a Mozart sonata in a competition, but for two reasons the day was not a success.

Earlier that morning, as we left our hotel to walk to the concert hall, my mother had received a telegram from the War Office informing her that her beloved younger brother Levin was missing, presumed killed in his Hurricane over France. She bravely insisted that the performance was to go ahead, and that she would come to it. Glimpses of her tear-stained face in the auditorium did nothing to aid concentration.

I was also interrupted in full flight by the judges, who told me that I was not to play repeats and that I had to start again. Between the two events it was scarcely a performance to challenge Horowitz, or any pianist in the competition for that matter.

Some years later I was to smash my thumb in the coal mines and this was, to my profound relief, to put paid to any fleeting and wholly illusory ideas I might have had of becoming a concert pianist. I might say I never could count – not even two against three – in which case it was from the start a ludicrous expectation.

I think I should add a small reflection on movie music. I have had my scripts accompanied, dramatically pointed up and occasionally drowned out or reduced to cliché by some of the world's most adroit composers. They range from Nino Rota in *Death on the Nile* to Cole Porter (arranged by John Lanchberry) in *Evil Under the Sun*.

In this latter task we were given the run of the Cole Porter estate in New England, where Lanchberry, a sort of poor man's Thomas Beecham, strolled around in a raccoon coat and a goatee beard, unearthing a great many of the master's gems, including quite a few wonders that had seldom been played, mainly I suspect because there were already too many numbers in the shows for which they had originally been composed. (Ethel Merman, for example, would close the score after eighteen numbers, a state of affairs somewhat different from the current Lloyd Webber musicals, where the score is mostly closed after one number endlessly reprised!)

I remember turning over a page of manuscript entitled 'I Concentrate On You'. I was able to read it because it was a simple piano line and not an entire orchestral score, like many of the others, which were beyond me. I said, 'This looks rather promising. Take a look.'

He crossed the room and had a peer. 'Promising?' he exploded. 'It's quite stunning! It's obviously the "Island Theme", the signature tune of the film.' (In fact 'I Concentrate On You' was never actually included in a stage production but was written for the film *Broadway Melody of 1940*, so technically it had not been ejected from a show.)

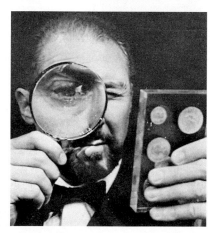

Scenes from the Broadway production of *Sleuth*.
Anthony Quayle and Keith Baxter.

Carolyn, me and Peter at the first-night party after the opening of *Sleuth*.

At the same party, me, Mrs and Mr Lennie Bernstein, Keith Baxter
and Anthony Quayle with the producer, Morty Gottlieb.

Truman Capote and Rex Reed bitching.

Conferences with the *Sleuth*
principals on set. Me and Larry
with Jolly Jack Tar eavesdropping
in the background ... and ...

Michael Caine, me, and the director, Joe Mankiewiecz.

Hitchcock, 'Please accept my Tony Award, Tony. Hitch.'
Another abominable pun from the old maestro.

Peter Ustinov as Hercule Poirot in *Death On The Nile*, in pensive mood.
The only bubble that could emerge from his mouth would be 'Sphinx!'

Dame Agatha Christie outside the St Martin's Theatre,
where she had been to see *Sleuth* with Marius Goring as Andrew,
which you can barely discern on the lit marquee behind her.
Look closely at her scarf!

The Royal Command film performance of *Evil Under the Sun*,
with between us in the background the movie's director, Guy Hamilton.
Asked by me whether she would leave if she suddenly remembered she
knew whodunit, she answered, 'I don't suppose they would let me!'

Richard Burton and me, the first morning on location of *Absolution* in Herefordshire
'No one plays Lear eight times in a week unless he's plumb crazy!'

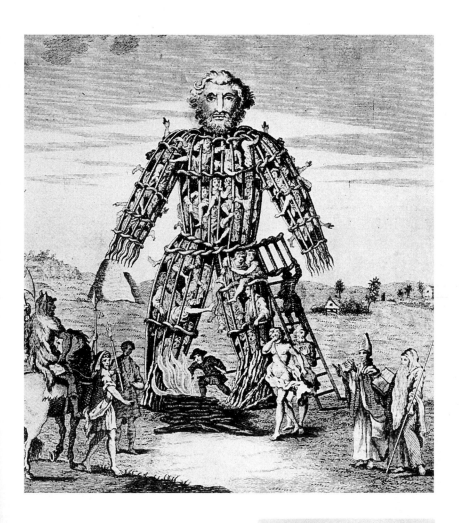

The eighteenth-century print on which the giant figure of the Wicker Man in the film is based.

All that remains of the Wicker Man today on Burrowhead – and of me!

The opening night of our Karnak Playhouse in the Jungle. Diane and me as Mr and Mrs FitzCarraldo.

Sir Peter waving a fond goodbye to the commonality after his investiture at Buckingham Palace, May 2001.

Its discovery, however, once enabled me to take a magnum of Louis Roederer champagne off a too-cocky cocktail pianist playing a 'Guess the Tune' medley in a Sydney hotel cocktail lounge.

'How did you know that?' he asked in a deeply aggrieved tone of voice, when I had guessed correctly. 'Most people have never heard of it.'

'Because I found it,' I replied grandiosely, explaining the circumstances.

'My dad always told me never to bet on a certainty,' he riposted gloomily. In the end we both split the price and the bottle.

One of the four Oscars awarded to the film of *Sleuth* was won by John Addison for, in my opinion, á rather feeble composition reminiscent of the kind of sub-standard, minor ballet stuff played by Leslie Bridgewater in the orchestra pits of many West End theatres in the 1950s to accompany anything from *King Lear* to *Charlie's Aunt*. On the other hand, entirely appropriate bombastic, imperial music, composed by the redoubtable Ron Goodwin, accompanied *Frenzy*, replete with sudden and menacing 'sting chords'. It fully supported the script in making the film important, inflated middle-cut Hitchcock.

Lanchberry's cunningly apposite arrangement undeniably raised the thirties-style quality of the film, which ended in the *Los Angeles Times* giving it one of the best reviews I've ever read in its columns, and led to the performance at Carnegie Hall of a glorious spoof suite, 'Porter Meets Poirot', conducted by the arranger himself.

The only other exceptional movie music I was involved with – other than the quite unique and extraordinary first movie score written for *The Wicker Man* by Paul Giovanni – was a piece I commissioned from the Master of the Queen's Music, the Australian-born Malcolm Williamson. We had met a number of times previously, chiefly at weddings and funerals – I was his best man with the not too easy job of keeping him steady and upright at the ceremony, and later he had turned up unexpectedly at my father's funeral to return the compliment. The movie in question was a lengthy documentary for RTZ (Rio Tinto Zinc) on the uses of that metal, directed with much flair and originality by my then partner Robin Hardy in England and Japan; it was lifted several notches further by Malcolm's elegiac music.

The history of the documentary is threaded with fine scores from exalted serious musicians – Bax, Holst, Walton, Vaughan Williams, Ireland, Britten – who all made their own contributions, as did the equally exalted poets Auden, Isherwood, Spender and Eliot, so I suppose I should have known what to expect.

Before leaving this musical chapter, I should perhaps interpolate a few words on Leonard Bernstein – a musical colossus, the only man effectively to join the classics with the modern (vide *West Side Story* and *Candide*) and whom I had the privilege of meeting on a number of occasions.

He was remarkable in so many ways that it is difficult to select what I personally found uniquely outstanding about him. *Au fin*, I think it must be his memory. Two illustrative stories will have to suffice.

The first concerns my meeting Lenny at his apartment in the Dakota Building in New York at a party he gave after a concert of Mahler's Eighth Symphony with the Israeli Symphony

Orchestra at Carnegie Hall – a performance notable for his energized control of pianissimo ('Lenny humping the music again' as my brother, Peter, remarked caustically as we left the venue). I was in the receiving line organized with regal splendour by the maestro, who had changed his post-concert kaftan three times already that evening. Though deeply busy with a hundred or more guests, and although we had not met for over two years, he immediately recognized me and demanded the punchline of a story I had been interrupted in telling, and had thus failed to supply at the previous encounter.

The next story is in some ways even more remarkable. It concerns a famous American pianist turned composer who sent Lenny the score of his first symphony for a critique. He heard absolutely nothing in reply, and had rather assumed that with his frantic global workload, the maestro had been too busy to look at it. Eighteen months later he was in Rome and saw Mr Bernstein striding gaily down the via Veneto in Rome. Plucking up the courage to approach the great man he introduced himself and with many apologies for interrupting his afternoon perambulation told him he was disappointed not to have heard his opinion of his First Symphony. 'But you've probably forgotten it,' he finished lamely.

'Not at all,' said Lenny, pausing for the briefest reflection, 'in the first movement you don't introduce your second subject till bar number 1,983, which is far too late, and I felt that the harp arpeggios in the slow movement were a trifle too skittish, particularly between bars 3,376 and 3,411, where you could have used some balancing sonorities in the cellos and basses.'

He continued in this vein analysing the scherzo and final movement, and with a swirl of his cape, a flourish of his stick, a lift of his hat, and an apology for his failure to communicate earlier, he was off down the avenue.

The composer collapsed into a café chair and watched him stroll away in wonderment.

'Was he right, do you think?' I asked him consolingly.

'That's not the point,' he said, 'what's amazing is he was accurate to a bar in a score he had only read through once all those many months before.'

That we will all remember Lenny just as accurately now that he has left us, I fully expect.

20. Theatre

The theatre was more to my taste than music. To tell the truth, on the whole I have found the company of musicians fairly detestable. They incline to the clannish and old maidish and their humour tends to be timid and fustian. And the great ones are tiresomely out of reach.

I suppose much the same thing can be said about actors – at least as far as the clannishness is concerned – but for the rest they are better company than most people: childish, affected, self-centred and with a 'camp' patina, even if they themselves are not homosexual.

My own small circle centred initially around the nucleus formed by the dancer and choreographer Johnny Heawood, the composers Peter Myers and Sandy Wilson in London, Julian Slade, John Morley and Simon Phipps at the Footlights in Cambridge, and Don Gemmel and Sachs at the Players Club under the arches at Charing Cross. My good friend Fenella Fielding was also a great one-woman draw for me at the time.

These friendly and familial influences apart, I was lucky to be just the right age to catch and appreciate the emerging giants of the British Theatre: Olivier, Richardson, Gielgud, Guinness, Redgrave, Evans, Ashcroft, Leigh, Thorndike et al., many of them playing together in the same exceptional company put together by the first two names in 1944 at the New Theatre, as it was then known, before it regrettably became the Albery. The range of plays was extraordinary: *Henry IV, Parts I and II, Richard III, Arms and the Man, King Lear, Peer Gynt, Oedipus* and *The Critic*, with Richardson giving us an incomparable Falstaff and Peer, and Olivier a quite sensational Richard and Oedipus and Mr Puff (*Oedipuff* as the evening came to be known). As Oedipus he of course gave vent to that visceral scream as he finally discovered the terrible truth about himself and tore his eyes out, which about caused the balcony to fall, as Ken Tynan remarks in his essay on that night; it certainly caused my neighbour, an elderly woman whom I didn't know, to fall across my knees in a dead faint. It was assuredly a tribute of a kind to the greatest actor of my time, and to a performance of unique athleticism that embraced and displayed every page of the actor's handbook. Those of us who still remember it − and his final exit *on* the divided curtain, somersaulting across the proscenium arch to end in a last fifteen-foot jump to the stage and a back-flip − form a kind of diminishing club, members of which I have met in many different parts of the world and who still speak of it in terms of hushed reverence.

Richardson's magisterial dottiness was less athletic although he partnered and matched Olivier every step of the way, his huge back supporting him up the stairs at the end of *Richard III* as the latter's helmeted head clashed against the flagstoned stair-case.

These two bestrode the theatrical world like colossi. Only Gielgud, with his greater refinement, challenged them. Sir John of course had his own dottiness and is famous for his naive non sequiturs and confrontational gaffes. Speaking about an actor, called, let us say, 'dash–dash', he would say, 'He is almost as boring as dash–dash – not you, of course, dear boy, the other dash–dash!'

I remember one evening in a New York apartment, when his friend Martin, an excitable Hungarian, rattling like a curtain rail with slave bangles, stood furiously at the door, accusing finger pointing levelly at John as he entered.

'John,' he screamed, 'you haf murdered my durdles!'

'Oh, no, I'm sure I haven't done any such thing,' wailed John helplessly.

Relentlessly Martin pointed to a fish tank, where five tiny turtles had gone belly up.

'Useless to deny it,' he screeched. 'Zer are ze bowdies.'

Gravely John moved to view the grisly remains. 'I'm sure I didn't hurt them,' he stuttered. 'I don't even know how they work!'

After years of working with them, I suppose I don't really know how actors work. Essentially they're a secretive lot, who mostly conceal the mainsprings of their talent. They are also pretty scary. It's always disconcerting to meet the man or woman who has moved you to exaltation or tears a few seconds before, and to find them far from god-like in their seedy dressing-gowns, sprawled before their untidy dressing-tables. It's almost impossible to join up the two images.

How can you reconcile the personae of people who spend their whole lives pretending to be someone else? It can't be done, not even sometimes by the actors themselves. Olivier told me that he once had an identity problem so severe that on stage in *The Master Builder* he did not know who he was. 'You mean what part you were playing?' I prompted.

'No,' he insisted. 'I mean I didn't know who *I* was.'

Too much overwork on and off the stage; too many roles, too many lines. Too many fictions. So what did he expect?!

In more modern times, needless to say, the theatre has become less exalted, more prosaic, minimalist and didactically over-preoccupied with conformist social conscience, so much so that, as far as censorship is concerned, political correctness has now taken the place of the late scarcely lamented Lord Chancellor, and the willing suspension of disbelief is scarcely a necessary adjunct of play-going any more. In 'kitchen-sink' drama, it was not only the kitchen that sank, but the flavours as well. While George Devine at the Royal Court was establishing the 'right to fail', he was also establishing the right to emasculate and fail to entertain. It is sad to see this credo surfacing again thirty-odd years later in the recently reopened Royal Court. Immediate relevance to contemporary problems appears to be all.

Which puts me in mind of the day, late in her last administration, that I was asked to take Margaret Thatcher to see Eugene O'Neill's *A Long Day's Journey Into Night* at the Haymarket. I was requested to do so by the theatre's owner, Duncan Weldon, the West End's most prolific producer ('Last year I put on more plays in this town than the National Theatre and the Royal Shakespeare Company combined,' he once said to me).

As if this wasn't daunting enough, the lead in the five-hour epic was, quite improbably, the comedy actor Jack Lemmon, a man of many accomplishments, I speculated, but surely somewhat lightweight for this titanic tragedy. Furthermore, Thatcher herself was not noted for her aesthetic sensibilities or her adherence to the drama; she had recently cut the grants to both the Royal Shakespeare Company and the National Theatre. Perhaps, I thought, this might be an opportunity to address her on this very subject, and anyhow a chance to meet such an august figure should not be missed. With these misgivings I accepted.

Many of the misgivings were unhappily realized. Lemmon, though gallant and energized, was entirely insufficient, and the PM ran entirely true to form. She sat bolt upright through the whole sempiternal performance, and when at the end I asked her how she had liked it she turned to me and barked brusque, military-style questions to which I was required to give cross/tick answers, as follows:

'Lemmon's character is a miser — right!?'

'Absolutely.'

'And his wife's a drug-fiend — right?!'

'No question of it.'

'Well, I've only got one question for you. Where did she get the money to buy the drugs?'

It was useless to expostulate that the drug was laudanum and very cheap at the time, or to point out that there was much more to the play than that. She simply wasn't interested, being entirely focused on the subject of drugs.

'There you are!' she snapped. 'Cheap drugs. That's the chief problem facing my government today!'

It was quite clear that she hadn't understood anything at all of O'Neill's major purpose in writing the play.

But later, at dinner in the back room (for security purposes) of the Mirabelle restaurant in Curzon Street, she showed her true mettle. Our party had by now increased to eighteen, including her husband Denis and Jack Lemmon.

At the start of the meal she asked everyone what they were doing and what their current aspirations were. At the end of it she shook everyone's hand, remembered their names and hopes, and wished them well with them. At 2 a.m., with a final regal wave of the hand she announced she had a cabinet meeting at 6 a.m., just as she had had the day before, and she had to leave us. Her final statement was a neatly turned witticism.

'I have to go now,' she said, 'if I don't want to make this a long night's journey into day!'

The great leaderene had lived up to expectations.

21. Practical Jokes

I've always been attracted to the practical joke. I suppose it's a legitimate extension of games-playing, though what an imprac-tical joke would be I couldn't guess. Perhaps simply one that cannot be made to work, or one that requires untold wealth to set it up? But what then is the true object of it? Pure glee is an obvious answer: so is vindictiveness, and so is correction. The checking of pomposity or ambition or vanity are obviously laudable objectives, and as long as they are brought off with reasonable wit and discretion and do no permanent harm we will approve and applaud them. The apotheosis of this kind of hoaxing I suppose took place in the programme of *Sleuth*, where we listed a number of actors who did not appear.

April Fool's Day is, of course, the traditional licensed jape day, and I myself have used it rather well on at least two occasions.

The first was when I was working at Charles Lytle's advertis-ing agency and decided to take down a peg a particularly pompous account executive who worked the ex-army officer routine a touch mercilessly – retained rank in civilian life, monocle, MCC tie, timewarp expletives – the lot.

At that time the great hoofer Jack Buchanan's wife, Susan, was acting as Charlie Lytle's secretary. When I came in that morning she said to me, 'You know it's April Fool's Day, don't you? Who's the mark?'

'Major Richmond,' I replied without thinking (not, by the way, his real name).

'And what's the gag?' Susan added.

'Haven't the faintest idea,' I said. 'Let's have a think. Perhaps the *Telegraph* might suggest something,' I added, reaching for the morning's newspaper.

A brief perusal suggested a pretty decent wheeze. A memorial service for a Captain G. B. Olley in a remote church in south-east London indicated gleeful possibilities.

'Suppose,' I suggested, 'that the good Captain Olley had been a good friend of Charlie Lytle – that he had known him on the Black and White whisky account' – which the agency handled – 'and that Charlie had always been devoted to the Olley family.'

'It's certainly a possibility,' she conceded. 'What happens next?'

'Well, wouldn't he want someone to represent this agency at the dolorous ceremony? Not some scruffy underling or ink-stained scrivener such as myself, but someone with the necessary poise and dignity, even military bearing, who would be a master of formality.'

Her face cleared. 'You mean?'

'Of course,' I said. 'The Major! He's absolutely perfect for it! All you have to do is send him a memo on Charlie's notepaper – you know the sort of thing: "I'm sorry about this, and I know it's a frightful bore, etc., but the old man's asked me to ask you whether you could possibly find the time to represent the agency at a memorial service to a great friend of his at eleven o'clock today at St Bede's Church, Southwark, or wherever. It's going to be pretty formal, I'm afraid, but I suppose a man of your background probably knows what's required." You know the sort of thing. Lay it on a bit thick and he's yours.'

'Leave it to me,' Susan grinned, disappearing back to her office.

Half an hour later the Major himself appeared in person in the office I shared with Rex Berry, fellow writer, attempted bigamist, wing three-quarter for the Wasps and genial, feckless friend.

'You chaps may be all right at scribblin' and that sort of malarkey,' he barked, 'but when it comes to carryin' off a serious occasion with style and a bit of spit and polish, who's called on – eh what?'

'Obviously you,' we chorused. 'But what can you mean?'

'Memorial service – great friend of the old man. Agency needs a representative, and I'm the one he's chosen!'

Obviously Susan had done her work well.

'Congratulations,' we said fulsomely. 'But you know, you can't go along in those clothes.'

'I think I know the required togs for a show like this,' he replied stiffly, and stalked off to Moss Bros to acquire the relevant threads.

Fate was on our side at the remote church. It was not a twenty-minute lick-and-a-promise job, but a full two-and-a-half-hour Catholic mass.

The Major arrived and greeted the uncomprehending widow with the news that he was representing Mr Lytle, who had known her husband on the Black and White whisky account.

'Whisky account?!' she said frostily. 'He was a life-long tee-totaller and Temperance Minister. What can you mean?'

The Major, somewhat baffled, scurried away into the church and fell to his prayers. And so he remained on his knees for two and a half hours in a remote church in south London, reverencing the memory of a complete stranger.

Much later that day he struggled back to the agency in full funerary fig, observed by the entire staff since, on the American pattern, all the walls of the offices were made of glass.

'Strange friends the old man has,' he fumed bleakly. 'No one there seemed to know him. Still, I suppose I'd better go and tell him that his friend was properly seen off.'

Realizing that it was probably most unlikely that Charlie would appreciate one of his top executives spending most of his working day in the aforementioned manner, and that my own job would very likely to be on the line, I thought that this was an apt moment to end the prank.

'Major,' I said hastily, 'I really must thank you most sincerely on behalf of the entire agency for the truly remarkable figure you have cut today. No one here could have brought it off like you . . . I only hope you will be prepared to perform the same dignified duties for us next – April Fool's Day.'

His face didn't go white or red before he stormed off – it went black. It is a tribute to the man that ten minutes later he returned, perfectly composed and in pretty good humour.

'I must say, that was very well brought off,' he said, extending a hand. 'Very well brought off indeed. I suppose I deserved that!'

It gives me the greatest pleasure to record that he and I have been the fastest friends ever since.

Even though he had sworn to be on guard and foolproof, I caught the same fellow exactly a year later on the next April Fool's Day. He had by this time opened his own firm and moved into some very smart premises in Mayfair with, as the estate agents would have it, 'a wealth of exposed polished pine walls and genuine Adam fireplaces'.

Luckily the date chosen for the opening was April 1st and quite a lot of work had to be done by me in order to keep it. Numerous Rowton houses (doss-houses) in central London had to be visited with leaflets promising free food at the Mayfair address on that date. The only stipulation was that the down and outs had to bring their own eating irons.

I had taken a room opposite, on the other side of the street from the posh new offices, and settled down to await the fun.

Promptly at noon the raggle-taggle army started to arrive, filing up the staircase into the newly furnished offices, mashing down the fresh lime-green Wilton carpet with their filthy iron-shod boots and banging their knives and forks on their plates and demanding food. When it became obvious that there was to be no grub, they turned these weapons on the 'wealth of exposed polished pine walls and genuine Adam fireplaces'.

Clearly visible through the window, I could see my distraught friend trying vainly to quiet the rioting mob. At the height of the mêlée, I telephoned to wish him a happy April Fool's Day and to suggest he look across to the window opposite. He did so and his maddened eyes locked on mine as I lifted a glass of something chilled and remedial in a triumphant gesture.

Clearly the down and outs could not be disappointed, and I had made provision for a mobile food kitchen to arrive at the spot shortly afterwards. The crowd of hoboes made an even greater mess with their bowls of soup and sausage rolls, which they insisted on consuming in the new offices as promised.

Five japes on a smaller scale will complete this list of comparatively harmless and benign escapades. The first concerns my brother Brian when he was about ten, we the twins thirteen. Over many months we sought to persuade him of the existence of scores of palpable untruths – that, for example, cans of tomato soup grew on trees, or that a certain breed of cow existed equipped with antlers, or that some dogs had gossamer wings. When these and many other equally maddening statements were challenged, they were all said to exist in a village in Tibet – 'the Village of the Ribbles'.

When proof of this wholly illusory village was demanded, we promised to send off for it. Peter and I set to work to fabricate it in its many wonders. Using fairly primitive forms of special effects to construct our photographs, we enclosed them in an envelope and, franking it with a Tibetan stamp from a stamp album, addressed it to Brian, mixing it in with the morning post. The results were equally gratifying parts of disbelief and fury.

The second concerns a very good friend of my brother Peter, Robert Leonard, a keen botanist, ornithologist and celebrated voice teacher (the American soprano, June Anderson, being one of his most glittering pupils).

He had bought and was earnestly cultivating a Japanese bonsai garden with dwarf trees artistically growing round a midget bridge over a mirror and picayune shrubs of all kinds.

One evening in a restuarant I had been served a sprig of

broccoli that very closely resembled a miniature oak tree. This I artfully placed by the side of the bridge, where it fitted quite beautifully into the scale of things.

The next morning Robert was all excited, calling everyone to witness the miracle growth that had occurred overnight because of his informed ministrations. My advice to him, naturally, was simply to put some Hollandaise sauce on it and have it for breakfast. He was not too pleased.

The third little jape was at my brother Peter's expense. It resulted, though it might be impossible for the reader to believe, from a stupid mistake of my own about the west window in the parish church in Rendham, Suffolk.

It was made of clear diamond-shaped panes of glass. Peter was enchanted with it, praising its beauty and great age. I disagreed about its age, claiming it to be of much more modern parentage, and a bet ensued to be settled by reference to Pevsner, the great expert on English church architecture. Unfortunately he failed to support me, and instead pronounced the window very fine and dating from the sixteenth century. I was of course furious, and Peter was triumphant, and furthermore not at all inclined to drop the subject. He continued the war dance for a further two months, repeating it every time we passed the church, which was quite often as we went by on the way to a friend in the area who was kind enough to invite us frequently for weekends. Something had to be done and a shaming hoax of some kind seemed to be indicated as a way to stop the sneering.

Fortunately, on one weekend when Peter was not down and I had gone by myself, I noticed that the window had scaffolding round it. This suggested a splendid wheeze. I got my friend to invite Peter for the following weekend while in the meantime I prepared a statement headed 'West Window Demolition Fund', which went on to say 'that research had shown that the window was a poor late-nineteenth-century copy created by the famous French church architect Francois Faux-Fenêtre', which had curiously led the famous Professor Pevsner into error. The demolition had already started but was expensive, and contributions were solicited and a suitably labelled contribution box provided. My friend placed the relevant document on the table in the church next to the contribution box, which she labelled appropriately while I took Peter off for a drink to a neighbouring pub.

The whole thing nearly went wrong on account of Peter's poor eyesight. He failed to notice both the paper and the labelled box until his attention was virtually forcibly drawn to them.

Initial dismay was replaced by mirth as he came to the name Faux-Fenêtre and he shot me an appreciative but suspicious look. With such an obvious name, he had got it, as I had intended him to! Obviously, these games are intended for glee – as loving presents, not for psyche-stripping humiliation fests – which is why the name was appreciated. But he very nearly didn't see it at all! Such is fate.

The next joke was more of a professional than a practical one, perpetrated on Jonathan Routh's highly ingenious television show *Candid Camera* with the help of his assistant Jennifer Patterson. Jennifer was a good and loyal friend for many years. A fervent Catholic with a compulsive sense of duty, she always managed to call me on my birthday, no matter where I happened to be in the world. She was a stout performer in every sense of the word, who later achieved remarkable success with her cooking programme *Two Fat Ladies* for the BBC. She unfortunately died suddenly and prematurely, and this tale is by way of being an affectionate epitaph to her driving spirit and never ending jollity.

The main problem I always felt with *Candid Camera* was that the jokes really had no place to go – for example, once the mechanic had discovered that the car cunningly rolled into his garage forecourt had no engine, he had nothing to do and nowhere to go but scratch his head in bewilderment.

I suggested to Jonathan that it might be possible to avoid this in-built diminuendo in the episodes by scripting them. He agreed to give it a try and, bearing in mind Jennifer's command of Italian and equally commanding presence, I set about devising an amusing comedy of errors.

We found a man who, though he spoke no Italian, had been conducting a highly successful and enterprising exchange of romantically slanted letters with an Italian lady who spoke no English but had had them translated in Italy by a friend. After a while he had persuaded her to visit him in England so that both could view each other and she could also view his London house – in short, object matrimony.

I really cannot imagine how this relationship was going to prosper unless one or both of them were to pay a visit to the Berlitz School of Languages. It was certainly to have even less chance after they had both encountered the formidable Miss Patterson at London Airport.

For example, he would say, 'She is even more beautiful than I had imagined she would be,' and this would be translated by

Jennifer as, 'He says that with your abundance of flesh you need not fear the English winters.' (The translation was subtitled on the screen in English.)

The Italian lady bridled considerably, and his surprised attempts to mollify her were similarly mistranslated, slowly increasing the insult. Descriptions of his property were naturally treated the same way. 'I have a spacious, detached house with a lovely garden, centrally located,' became 'He says he has a modest, two-roomed flat in a housing estate on the outskirts of London, but it is very serviceable.' And per contra, her modest demands were grossly inflated. 'Tell him I will be quite satisfied with only a few local shops,' was translated as 'She says she can't wait to go to Harrods, and Fortnum and Mason, of which she has heard so much.'

Things of course went from bad to worse, he thinking he had got hold of a top-drawer gold-digger, and she assuming she had come to marry an insulting, poverty-stricken suburbanite.

All bets were off as they glared resentfully at each other, insults and curses flying, until we decided to reintroduce Cupid by telling them that they were on *Candid Camera* and that it was all a joke.

I'm not sure, however, that they looked at each other ever again in quite the same way, having had a glimpse of something very different from what had been expressed in their letters.

The last prank concerned Phyllis, Lady Cilento and her daughter Diane. They often sparred together in a sportif manner, the latter mainly taking the role of scamp and court jester to the sovereign Phyllis.

She complained one day that her mother had never really

known who she was (as she was the runt of the large litter), forgetting her name on most days.

As a result I challenged her to a bet — that she couldn't call on her mother and spend an hour or so in her company without the old lady detecting who she was. The stake was a case of Château d'Yquem.

Disguised only in a hideous spotted shift and fright wig, with a fearful déclassé accent, she actually managed to persuade her mother that she was a shop girl with the ludicrous name of Babs Husseybuzzy who had won a prize on television to play her daughter Diane in a film of her life. She had come along seeking biographical background on which to base her performance.

Her mother was appalled by the crude brat in front of her, but nonetheless swallowed the bait hook, line and sinker. In this she was helped by some wicked confirmatory details about Miss Husseybuzzy from me. I followed a preparatory phone call with a visit to the house a few minutes before Diane made her entrance, warning Phyllis of the frightful ordeal she was shortly to undergo from the dreadful, importuning supplicant.

'I'm afraid she won't take no for answer,' I said. 'She's quite ghastly, and has been making our lives a misery for days. But if you are good enough to see her briefly it will get her off our backs and help Diane enormously, etc., etc.'

In the event, Diane got more than she had bargained for. Her mother launched herself with great relish into a catalogue of her daughter's life-long peccadilloes and insufficiencies.

Somewhat chagrined, Diane abruptly let her mother off the hook, whereupon she feigned to have recognized her all along and to be just having some sport with her. As this was patently not the case, I had to pay up for the wine — most of which, however, I contrived to drink myself. So what did you expect?!

But the boot is not always on one foot in this world. Some years ago, to the discomfiture of my guests, I played a successful adaptation of a party murder game invented by Stephen Sondheim in and around my Somerset schoolhouse. One of those guests was the stage director Peter Wood, and he totally fooled me into believing that a horrible act of violence had been committed in an evilly lit chamber at the top of some winding stone stairs in a neighbouring Gothic dwelling.

It was of course a total fabrication – he had arranged quite beautifully to get even for other puzzlements and hoaxes practised on him by myself. Perhaps only to be expected.

The party murder game is perhaps worth a brief description on account of its inherent ingenuity as a game (not all of which will be revealed here), its ability to accommodate any number of guests, and the fact that it embraces both the logical and the spooky. In addition, of course, it affords abundant opportunities for dalliance in the dark.

A room is elected a safe room, where, on a table, lies a quantity of numbered envelopes. Inside all except one of the envelopes are instructions as to where you have to go to find your clue, which you then have to fetch at great peril of your life and bring back to the safe room.

In the excepted envelope is the message 'You are the murderer' and a description of the whereabouts of the murder weapon. This individual must 'kill' as many people as possible by grasping them by the neck and proclaiming, 'I am the murderer – give me your clue!'

Having surrendered their photographic clues, victims as well as those who have managed to escape the killer's clutches now return to the safe room, along with the murderer. All can then play at naming him. Obviously, all who have been assaulted by him and robbed of their clues can recognize and point to him, but this will do them no good, as they have to prove it. This infallibly *can* be done by a close study of the photographic clues, which together show a complex pattern, and the employment of deductive and inductive logic. The process will be easier or more difficult in direct proportion to the number of photographic clues on display. The more successful the murderer has been in his slaughtering and robbing, the fewer clues there will be on view. As a result more pieces of the pattern will be missing, and thus it will be commensurately the more difficult to identify him.

I once devised this game for a house party in the country hosted by stage producer Michael White, using my daughter Claudia as the tomato-ketchup-stained 'victim' in the all-important photographs. Her moribund poses were so disturbingly effective that they spooked out not only her mother at home, but also the woman at the party who had drawn the murderer card, so that she stood paralysed in the dark driveway of the house, quite failing to kill anyone. As a result I had to call it all off and start another game, which luckily for me went with a great swing. The night resounded with satsfying shrieks of one kind and another, and it ended with one of the guests – I rather think it was Keith Baxter – solving the problem after a gratifying mental tussle.

Less amused by this game was my brother Peter when he played it in New York under the direction of its inventor, Stephen Sondheim.

So What Did You Expect?

He was sent upstairs to a remote, dimly lit bathroom to find his clue, only to discover the star of *Psycho*, Anthony Perkins, waiting for him behind the shower curtain. He just about jumped out of his skin, as had been planned, but knowing the wily and wicked Steve as he did, he should have expected it.

22. A Few Random Tales

Olga Detterding was one of the most eccentric figures I ever met and certainly the richest. She also managed to put me into the strangest position I've ever been in – that of being able to bring down a British government!

She was the Shell Oil heiress, and at one time her income was claimed to be over £1 million an hour, so she should not have been worried by the comparatively trivial sums of money that this story concerns.

The whole thing started at her penthouse apartment opposite the Ritz overlooking Piccadilly, where we had foregathered to watch the Queen's fireworks; it was a distinguished throng including, I remember, S. J. Perelman, Jonathan Routh, her lover at the time, and the Baron Philippe de Rothschild, who was wearing what he called his '*jabot feu d'artifice*', a strange velvet jacket covered in tiny gold-sprigged explosions to represent fireworks. One has to be fairly impressed with a man who has a special coat in which to watch fireworks.

Olga, who significantly was imbibing copiously, asked me whether I had ever been inside 10 Downing Street, where she was going on the morrow – a Sunday – to a lunchtime cocktail party after the Trooping of the Colour. I said I hadn't but was very interested to see what lay behind that slightly sinister door, so often seen on television half opening to admit cantankerous supplicants and petitioners. She kindly invited me to join her.

As it turned out the party was at No. 11, the residence of the Chancellor of the Exchequer, and it was in full swing by the time I arrived the next day.

As I did so, an overexcited Olga lurched up to me and pointed to a man, Willie Peploe, who was just leaving.

'There goes the Catholic censor,' she boomed at me. 'You know, of course, he banned your brother Peter's play *Equus*?'

'What on earth for?' I asked. 'There is nothing in the play to incite Catholic disapproval.'

'Oh yes there is,' she persisted. 'In the penultimate scene a phallic-shaped object is placed on the crucifix.'

I told her that that was the merest nonsense and that there was no such thing in the piece, a play I knew very well and had actually not only seen many times but read equally many times in its various versions, including the very first original manuscript.

But Olga would have none of it. In strident tones she pursued me round the room, which was full of the nation's political glitterati, finally reducing it to silence. She screeched at me that I was a complete idiot who didn't know what I was talking about and that the matter was as described by her. She then invited me to bet with her on the subject. I declined, saying rather smugly that I had been taught never to bet on a certainty.

'Coward!' she howled in the still quietened room, at which point, in order to keep the peace, I agreed to a modest wager of

£1,000 or so. She repeated the epithet and suggested a stake of £250,000. Again I tried to dissuade her, but she was adamant and led the way next door into No. 10, into the Prime Minister's private office in fact, in search of paper on which to record the bet.

I should pause here to point out that the Prime Minister of the day was Callaghan and that his government had a majority of one in the House of Commons. Two other factors are relevant: a vote of confidence was to be held on the following Wednesday, and a rash of leaks had undermined confidence in our security systems. What was happening in the PM's private office in Downing Street, when he was away from it on a Sunday, was therefore a matter of great sensitivity.

What almost certainly he would not have welcomed was the scene that was actually taking place there – a multi-millionairess, high on some prohibited substance, since she wasn't drinking that day, rummaging through his desk unchecked to find a sheet of paper on which to record the following bet: 'I, Olga Detterding, bet Anthony Shaffer the sum of £250,000' – subsequently, with a final accusation of cowardice, doubled and initialled – 'that in the play of *Equus* there is a phallic-shaped object placed on the crucifix.'

The whole faintly squalid scene and documentation was witnessed by a senior member of the House of Commons and signed by we three, and we all returned to No. 11.

I pocketed my copy and was about to leave when the full truth of the matter dawned on me. I turned and said to Olga, 'It's a pity it's a Sunday and the theatres are closed. If they were not you would be able to walk up Whitehall into Charing Cross Road, where at Wyndham's Theatre you would be able to see a play called *Once A Catholic,* in which such a scene as you ascribe to *Equus* actually takes place featuring some naughty schoolgirls, a crucifix and a banana. Goodbye, and thanks for the use of the hall!'

I started to stroll out, but she followed me, screeching like a demented creature, 'That's what I meant of course . . . It was a slip of the tongue, that's all. *Once A Catholic* not *Equus* . . . *Once A Catholic* not *Equus* . . . *Once A Catholic* not *Equus* . . .'

The next day I sent her a copy of both plays, with the relevant passage marked in *Once A Catholic,* along with a request for a cheque for half a million pounds.

The request fell on stony ground. After a repeated missive, I finally received a letter from her solicitor, warning me to stop hassling their client and pointing out that the bet was unenforceable at law on premises where alcohol was being consumed. Not only was this untrue – vide the Clermont Club, et al. – but it seemed curious to me that the one who was sober and whose judgements could not be affected by booze should invoke this arcane law against the other party to the bet, who *was* drinking.

In the event I didn't get paid and the lady most regrettably choked to death shortly afterwards on a piece of meat, but in view of the above I had been placed in a most sinister and invidious position, with the unquestionable power to publish the account of the Sunday in Downing Street and bring down the, for me, detested socialist government the following Wednesday.

I consulted my agent, Kenneth Ewing, who advised me to have a word with a mutual friend, and coincidentally advisor to

Callaghan, the Labour life peer and guardian of the nation's secrets Lord Goodman.

I did so and he concurred that without doubt the account of the shenanigans in Callaghan's office over the weekend, if published, would certainly bring him down. But he advised me to hold my hand.

'If you use your information,' he said, 'the Special Branch would make life intolerable for you in the future. For example, your car would be continually ticketed and impounded, you would be strip-searched every time you passed through customs, and all manner of steps would be taken to make your life in England a misery.'

'You would say that,' I countered. 'Wilson was your master. He gave you your title. You plainly want his successor to succeed.'

'You don't have to believe me, but I don't actually want that,' he said rather surprisingly. 'Still, it's up to you to evaluate. It just depends on how much you care about living here.' He gave me one of his expansive smiles. 'But if I were you, I would do as I say. It's unnecessary to do anything. I can assure you that the government will fall on Wednesday – by one seat.'

He was absolutely right, and I think pleased with it. The only person who got nothing out of it – neither riches, nor the reputation of being a power-broker – was me, though I did hold the balance for the very briefest of moments.

So what do you expect from a legal and political Machiavelli and a multi-millionairess?

That episode still haunts me as an example of how amazingly easy it is to manipulate the reins of power.

Another haunting incident happened a little time later in the George V Hotel in Paris, where I had gone with Kenneth Ewing to meet the film producer Carlo Ponti.

After dinner, and a brief sight of his impossibly beautiful wife Sophia Loren, and an opaque and fairly baffling conversation about the project that concerned us, I returned to my suite — grand chambers stuffed with all manner of boule escritoires, chests of drawers, marble-top sidetables and a wealth of gold ormolu knick-knackery.

Wearily I sank on to the bed and turned the lights off. Immediately a voice spoke in the darkness, 'The body is mine!'

Frozen with horror but nonetheless excited to be in the middle of my first real-life (if one can use such words) ghost story, I restored the light and looked around. Nothing untoward was to be seen. The implacable gilt neutrality of the room stared back — a dead room like all hotel rooms, doing its best to add to the atmosphere of unease and isolation.

I switched off the lights and returned to bed. Immediately I heard the sepuchral words, 'No, the body is mine.'

I instantly jumped to my feet again, and again examined the room without success.

These events were repeated three more times until I was pretty badly scared and called Kenneth on the phone to join me.

I was half afraid this spectral manifestation wouldn't occur while he was present, and indeed for a while it did not. Total silence reigned, and looking significantly at the glass of cognac by my bedside, he made for the door.

Despondently I sat on the bed, and at that moment the voice

spoke, 'You shall not have the body. I tell you it is mine to dispose of.'

We exchanged mixed looks – of triumph on my part and fear on his.

'Now you must believe me,' I said as we embarked on a new search of the room.

Eventually we discovered what was taking place. I very much regret it owed nothing to the spirit world.

My bed was the trigger for a loose connection in a speaker concealed in a seventeenth-century bureau; my weight simply set it off. Years before, in the thirties, when the Georve V was built, mainly to accommodate English visitors, it had incorporated a radio system that was stocked with readings of English classics. One of them was Dickens's *Our Mutual Friend*, the opening chapter of which concerned the retrieval of bodies from the River Thames. It was to this we were listening. So no first encounter with a genuine haunted room! Just a pedestrian and mechanical explanation, I'm afraid.

Among other ludicrous and embarrassing plots – so beloved of tacky TV shows – was the time I was trapped between floors in a lift in the Saint Regis Hotel in New York in the company of Ned Sherrin and Salvador Dalí.

Two more or less pukka Englishmen, determined to show no signs of alarm or apprehension, were flanked by a frenetic Spaniard whose waxed, pointed moustaches took up almost all the available space and whose hysterical imprecations – 'Mama Mia, all is lost, it is finished, and no priest present!' – took up the available air.

Upright his moustaches pierced our cheeks, noses and ears; on his supplicating knees, they pierced our calves and ankles.

Our companion chose to ignore the clear signs of rescue echoing from without. He continued to scream for help from a priest until the roof finally burst open and an Irish workman thrust his head in and said, 'You won't be needing one of them just at the moment. You can all climb out.'

A solution to our dilemma, which all the time I'd quite obviously expected.

23. Health

It may well be the time now to indulge the family taste for hypochondria. I do not believe I will be quite the adept that my brother Peter has managed to become – he has been known to claim to have my illnesses as well as his own – but it must be said in his defence that last year he did have a triple bypass operation and made light of it. In a tit-for-tat piece of legerdemain, I think in this case I can claim a spookier experience.

Paying a visit to the intensive care unit, I failed to report to the matron on duty but went instead to my brother's curtained bedside. There he lay, marble-white and freezing cold, with no detectable sign of breathing or pulse. I ran to the nurses' station yelling, 'Quick my brother is dead,' and quoted the above certain signs of death.

I received in return a pitying look and a severe lecture on not reporting first to the desk, and was then accompanied back to the bedside, where, to my considerable relief, monitors concealed behind a curtain were pointed out. All showed perfectly normal readings. It was also carefully explained that the body is chilled before the operation – hence the cadaver-like temperature – and that with the heart temporarily outside the body there is no pulse.

The second shock I had recieved was – because of the twin-like mirror images – seeing myself as *I* would look on my own deathbed. A salutary lesson!

Most of my life has been quite free from serious illness, until the late eighties, when I developed a benign brain tumour, which sat on the fossa of the pituitary and had to be removed because it threatened my sight. The resulting operation was performed at the Middlesex Hospital by a surgeon called Mr Andrews, who was furious I had secretly left the place the night before the operation to visit L'Étoile restaurant round the corner in Charlotte Street in order to say farewell to a number of vintages, as it had been forecast I might not be able to smell again after the operation.

In the event, I did in fact, lose my sense of smell, as well as the sight of my right eye. One day, owing to possible revolutionary developments in science, the former might be reparable, but I somehow doubt it; unfortunately Andrews, almost as if in revenge for the L'Étoile incident, cut the olfactory nerves too far apart to seek each other. The latter, I'm afraid, is irreparable.

My next run-in with a surgeon, in September 1997, came about as a result of my falling down a flight of dark slate steps. Being black and greasy and serrating easily, it is a ridiculous substance to create stairs out of, but that is nonetheless what in our wisdom we had used outside our house in Karnak in Australia. I skied down them early one evening, landing with a forbidding crack on my head.

I knew as soon as I had done it that I had accomplished more than a torn tendon and a bruise or two. There followed a swift visit to the Mossman cottage hospital, an institution of picayune charm, and in particular to their X-ray department, where a fossilized machine that had started life in the Palaeozoic era awaited me. To the dismay of my intern, who had forecast that I was to be a guest of the hospital for some months, the plates showed no break. It's a far cry from the courtesies and circumlocutions of Harley Street. He caused me a painful laugh when he summed up, 'Frankly, sport, I don't know what's holding yer fucking head on!'

Paraphrasing the precocious four-year-old Macaulay replying to an adult enquiry about an injury, the pain soon 'became much abated' and I thought no more about it.

Ten months later I started dropping things like plates and glasses. Diane suddenly said to me, 'What the hell's happened to your arm? You look like something out of Belsen.'

A look in the mirror confirmed that the deltoid muscle had almost entirely disappeared. The biceps, when flexed, closely resembled a quail's egg.

Something had to be done, so I went for a mercury scan in Cairns. The first thing I did was assure the man there that the one thing he needn't have to worry about was a broken neck, since I didn't have one. He gave me the kind of look you would accord somebody seriously deranged and pointed to a white line on the scan.

'You've got a break in it the size of the Great Divide,' he said. 'The way those neck bones are, I don't know why you're not dead! A fall from a pavement would see you off.'

It turned out that I also had a blockage in the central nervous system that was forecast to reduce me to a quadriplegic within a couple of years. So, after several more confirmatory opinions, I submitted myself to an operation by a Mr Crockard, which in effect reduced me for the time being to the quadriplegic status I was seeking to avoid. I was in a wheelchair for six months, and for nearly a year couldn't dress, bathe, feed myself, write or walk. These skills mercifully returned to me after many sessions of hydrotherapy, mostly at the Devonshire Hospital, where attractive but indefatigable experts laboured cheerfully to get things moving again. Initially there were many dark days, attended by oft-returning thoughts of *felo de se* and concomitant wonder at the multifarious and stubborn functions of the human body. No matter how hard one tried, it simply wouldn't do what one told it to do. What I was principally persuaded of, finally, was that I suspect very few people would opt to have an operation to avoid a hypothetical later disaster if they accurately knew what they were going to go through.

In this respect I should have known better as a result of my previous experience in the Middlesex Hospital. When I had the operation for the removal of the tumour in the head, the prognosis had been that it would expand as far as it could, blinding the left eye, and then return to blind the right one. With hindsight, I should have waited and seen if that's what it looked like doing. The great stage director Joan Littlewood, who had the identical condition, did just that on my recommendation and lived to win the day. She kept both her eyesight and her sense of smell for a decade or more. General Clausewitz, the great proponent of the theory of 'masterly inactivity', would most certainly have approved.

My operation, on the other hand, turned out to be something of a nightmare. I languished for six weeks in the archaic Middlesex Hospital, half sedated and entirely out of the game. At one point I had completely forgotten my name and recalled it by consulting the inside pocket of my jacket, where the Savile

Row tailors Anderson and Shepherd had with the greatest possible forethought inscribed it.

Another incidence of forgetfulness was not so easily solved. Every day a well-dressed woman full of concern would come and sit by my bedside. As the days passed I became increasingly touched by her sedulous behaviour and curious about her identity. The face was familiar but that was about as far as it went, so one day I simply came out with it.

'Would you be kind enough to tell me exactly who you are?'

There was a gasp and the sound of high-heeled shoes clacking sharply across the floor. If ever a hospital door can be said to have slammed, my door was the one. At any rate, it hissed virulently like a mutant python.

Moments later the nurse entered, in best firm nanny mode. 'Who's been a naughty boy, then?' she began surreally. 'What have you been up?'

'Naughty boy indeed!' I replied impatiently. 'Is it likely? I've been unconscious for a couple of months. As for that lady, I merely asked her who she was.'

'That was your *mother*!' she answered with more reptilian sibilance. At that moment I began to realize just how ill I had been. The net loss was the sight of my right eye and sense of smell. As I have indicated, the net gain was extremely questionable.

For the rest, my health has always been pretty good, though I did once receive a death sentence from a French doctor.

It came about in this way. Two weeks into a protracted holiday in France with Carolyn and my two girls, Claudia and Cressida, I was staying in a château-now-hotel in the French–

German border town of Scieux. You know the sort of place well, I suspect: gardens of manicured pot plants, armoured public rooms and tessellated vellum menus. On the first morning there I was lying in bed feeling so poorly that death would have been a welcome alternative. The manager entered with the last of the above mentioned objects and proceeded to read out its cream-clogged contents. I countered by groaning theatrically, and asked him if there were a doctor in the house.

'*Eh hélas, non,*' was the reply. But if I could get myself to the local village the best doctor in France awaited me. Somehow I managed to get myself down there. Once in his august and wintry presence, I graphically explained to him the nature of my malady. I also told him that I had never been ill in this particular way before and that this was something of a worry. (For example, 'flu may be miserable, but as long as you can recognize that that is what you have, it is bearable.)

He nodded sagely and proceeded to wheel in a Heath Robinsonian machine constructed of outlandish ancient cogs, wires and plates. Lights flashed and ratchets whirred and then he asked me to wait for about ten minutes.

On my return he had the face of a gravestone and assisted me into a chair as if I were a nonagenarian granny.

'*Hélas, c'est terminé,*' he groaned sepulchrally.

'*Terminé?*' I quavered.

'*Précisement. Vous avez un foie comme une balle de golf.*'

'Is that good?' I enquired hopefully.

'*Au contraire,*' he quickly disabused me. '*Vous avez six mois – au maximum!*'

A maximum of six months to live. Was there a chance he could be wrong?

Absolutely not. There was nothing left of the liver, thus confirming Freud's only known joke that life was up to the liver.

I reeled out into the tiny square, with its ordered plane trees, and numbly sat on a wooden bench. In a very short time my reactions became surprisingly the reverse of what you might have predicted. Whilst there was inevitably the heightening effect of shock, as a result of which I remember I saw every object around with enormous clarity – the grain of the wood on the bench, the pores of my own hand, the weave of my suit; there was also an enormous feeling of ecstatic relief which filled my whole being. 'Thank God,' I thought, 'I don't have to go off to Puerto Rico and make those dreary Coca-Cola commercials next week, or any other dreary commercials for that matter ever again.' I was liberated. I was free. I could do anything I liked! My only problem was how I was to fill the next six months. Was it, for example, to be with the Inca civilization, or the Egyptian etc., etc.? And I started to laugh hysterically.

What I had failed to realize was that my wife Carolyn had followed me down from the hotel and was lurking among the plane trees, observing me. When she finally emerged it was of course to ask, 'So, what did the doctor say?'

Since I had decided to keep the doleful news to myself, I replied, 'A touch of indigestion, that's all.'

'Bollocks,' I think was the crisp response from the unfoolable female. 'I've been watching you for quite a while, and your face has been a study of alternating sun and cloud – wild laughter and blank despair. Rather a strange reaction to indigestion, I'd have said.'

'Indigestion can be very alarming,' I said feebly.

'Out with it!' she replied implacably.

After a lot more toing and froing with increasing calorific content, we finally ended up having a major row, which irritated me profoundly.

'I'm the one who's got the death sentence,' I complained. 'And I'd managed to come to terms with it, until you came along and started carping.'

'But,' she said, 'you were laughing uproariously.'

'Well, to tell you the truth, I find it pretty funny.'

'Do you?' she answered glacially. 'Well, let's go back to the hotel and see how funny your kids find it.'

This incited me even more as being the work of a spoilsport. Finally we agreed to say nothing to them. Driving back to Blighty with a car full of howling kids wasn't my idea of joy.

Once back home I went to see my doctor, the stage medical advisor Patrick Woodcock. Now, with only five months to live, I thought, I had better pay his bill, which I had ignored for a couple of years. He was so surprised that I was forced to tell him the entire story. He became even more surprised.

'And you believe the French?' he asked incredulously. '*Balle de golf* indeed,' he snorted, wrestling with my eyelids, I presume to check for anaemia. 'I don't believe a word of it. I know a woman at St Thomas's Hospital who will soon sort this out. It's probably only a *crise de foie*!'

So off I went for a biopsy, counselling restraint in regard to the amount of liver removed.

'There's only a little golfball of it to start with,' I pointed out.

Two days later I got the good news from Patrick. He had a report on his desk from the woman at St Thomas's to this effect: 'Whilst Mr Shaffer does not have the liver of a ten-year-old child' – frankly I didn't know why I should have – 'and it shows evidence of some abuse, I cannot see how the French doctor could have come to the conclusion he did. With normal care and attention the patient should live out a normal term of years.'

'Marvellous,' I cried, my previous death wish having entirely disappeared. 'Let's go out and celebrate.'

Patrick gravely stemmed the enthusiasm. 'Whilst felicitating with you on your renewed term of years,' he said thinly, 'I have to draw your attention to the paragraph "Whilst Mr Shaffer . . ." I have been in your house on many occasions and I have seen you pour out the four-finger dark mahoganies' (his term for whisky and too little splash). 'They are doing you no good, old boy.'

'So here comes the commercial,' I said gloomily. 'Give up the booze – change to cherryade!'

'Don't be silly,' he riposted, 'I don't waste time telling people to do what I know they won't do. Change to white wine.'

'White wine before dinner,' I moaned. 'You can't be serious?'

'Never been more so,' he said, 'and you can always make it champagne. It's actually quite good for you. Now come along, swear you'll give up whisky for wine. And by that I mean all spirits – don't be a smart ass and just change to vodka or gin. I want to be drinking with you in twenty years' time, and that won't happen if you go on the way you are. You'll have five, more like – if that.'

He held out his hand. I might point out that Patrick himself was no mean toper and therefore obviously knew what he was talking about. His gravitas persuaded me to grasp the proffered hand and swear as demanded.

I have never gone back on it, and I'm sure it has been instrumental in keeping me in the ring, not that the habitual champagne-drinking has done a lot for my bank account, but it was hardly to be expected that it would!

24. 'Death of a Blood Sport'

Well, that's just about all I can remember. I have tried not to be the hero of every story, and not to be too castigatory of the failings of other people I have met along the way. And I have probably failed at both.

I have been lucky in most of these people, so many of them names eminently worth dropping, or offering friendships worth holding on to.

I have also been lucky in having been just in time to drink about the last of the *Sleuth* vintage wine that so amused me and finally served me so well on stage and screen. I don't think there's that much of it left. Perhaps the genre has just changed out of all recognition, as I wrote some years ago in an article for *Harpers' Bazaar* that I have no qualms about reproducing here to end with. It is called 'Death of a Blood Sport'.

It is arguable that no literary form has given us a longer, more intriguing, more fanciful run for our money, than the classic, closed-circle English detective story which flourished at its very best in the fifty years before the outbreak of the last world war.

Many people have tried to analyse just why it was that the detective story became so overwhelmingly popular during those years, but surely Arthur Machen came nearest to an explanation when he wrote: 'Man is so made that all his true delight arises from the contemplation of mystery, and save by his own frantic and invincible folly, mystery is never taken from him; it rises within his soul a well of joy unending.'

It helped of course that the rules of the game were relatively simple to learn, and all could play. The setting, for the most part, was an English country house with its study, gun-room, conservatory or library for the body to be discovered in; its blue rooms, green room, red rooms and turret rooms to sleep the suspects in; its sculleries and stone-flagged servants' hall for ferrety valets, orotund butlers and hysterical, half-wit parlourmaids, respectively to plot, pontificate and sniffle in; and its surrounding parkland, invariably impassable by reason of snow or flood to be lurked in. Allow the generator supplying the house with electricity to run down, and the snow or flood to destroy the telephone wires and/or bridge out of the place, and the board was set. 'My God, do you realize it has to be one of us?' screams one of the suspects, probably the murderer, and the game had well and truly started.

The counters were a half dozen or eight ill-assorted, highly improbable, cardboard figures – the Colonel, the Lawyer, the Spinster Aunt, the Ingénue, the Nephew from Australia, the Self-Made Man, the Unbalanced Playboy, the Famous Actress being recurring favourites. They would start out bluff, priggish, insouciant, demure, flamboyant or prim, according to their standardized

exteriors, and would be gradually broken down into so
many repositories of guilty secrets by the King Counter,
the Detective or Sleuth, and guilty secrets they all certainly
had. It will turn out, for example, that the Colonel was at
one time put on probation for soliciting policemen on
Hampstead Heath dressed only in frilly directoire knickers;
or that the Ingénue was, perhaps unwittingly in her case as
she may be needed for the clinch on the last page,
involved in an abortion ring run by a pitiless Levantine; or
again that the Spinster Aunt, when once involved as a
nanny, stabbed her infant charge with a poisoned button
hook. Never in life were weekend country retreats so
thronged with embezzling lawyers, cowardly commanders,
drunken doctors and baby-farming bankers. Half the fun
was knowing that every cupboard in the mansion
contained its skeleton.

The detectives who conducted these gruelling, not to
say unauthorized investigations came in various shapes and
sizes, but were for the most part either aristocratic,
eccentric or malformed. The fashion for dottiness started
right at the beginning with Poe, whose Auguste Dupin,
we are informed, had a habit of living behind closed
shutters illuminated by a couple of tapers which, strongly
perfumed, emitted only the ghastliest and feeblest of rays.
From this stronghold he issued by night to promenade the
streets and enjoy the 'infinity of mental excitement'
afforded by quiet observation. Sherlock Holmes, who
followed him, substitutes cocaine for candlelight, and adds
indoor pistol-practice and the violin; Baroness Orczy's
Old Man in the Corner knots string; Sax Rohmer's

Maurice Klaw irrigates his wits with a verbena spray and carries with him an 'odically stellilized' cushion to promote psychic intuition. Max Carrados is blind, Hercule Poirot has luxuriant moustachios and wears patent leather shoes, John Dixon Carr's Doctor Fell is so fat that he can scarcely walk, and Dorothy Sayers's Lord Peter Wimsey of Duke's Denver has a pretty taste in fine wines, Horace quotations and incunabula. Above all the Sleuth had to possess two qualifications – amateurism and an infallibility that would come to the rescue on those all too numerous occasions when it seemed that 'the best brains of Scotland Yard were baffled'.

The moves in the game were made by casting suspicion on all the characters in turn, finally selecting as the murderer the Least Likely Suspect, and no one was exempt from this category. Dwarves; nonagenerian seamstresses; infants; prime ministers; jurors at the trial of the wrongly accused man; the counsel for the prosecution; deaf mutes; paralysed jobbing gardeners; entranced Hottentots; Pomeranian sopranos; the detective himself; and the actual narrator of the story. Ironically the person who seems to have done it least of all is the Butler, perhaps because he became from the start the Most Likely Suspect.

Anything would do as a weapon, and the more bizarre the better. Victims were stabbed with ice daggers which then melted; garden implements, sharpened druid crosses and astrolabe arrows. They were shot with cross-bows from Crécy and arquebuses from the Armada. Poisoned bloater paste, galoshes and false teeth sent them into

rictuses, while Gutenberg bibles, Carmelite collection
plates and Renaissance clock weights clouted them into
the next world. Similarly obscure devices for
electrocution, strangulation, ashpyxia, defenestration and
embolic despatch were also freely employed. In each case,
of course, points were scored by the Sleuth for identifying
the weapon or recognizing the cause of death. 'It seems to
me that Lord Rokebey died from a clod of cudweed
blasted up the left nostril by this Orinoco nose flute,' the
detective will opine nonchalantly and not surprisingly no
one will have the courage to gainsay him.

The game ended with the dénouement or revelation
scene, in which all the suspects are called into the drawing
room and, having meekly agreed, are treated to a lengthy
reconstruction of the crime by the detective. There were
usually twenty or so pages of complex dialogue, which
was for the addict the veritable heart of the artichoke, the
filet mignon of the bull. It would go something after this
fashion: 'It's really quite easy when you come to think of
it. Dr Sedgewick was never in London at the time of the
murder. In fact the good doctor stayed in a small hotel in
Melksham on the night of the 7th, then returned next day
to Broughton Gifford on the 2.40 train, disguised as
Charles Stockley's valet Burcon, whom he knew had a
grudge against his master and had been overheard in the
servants' hall threatening to kill him. He made sure he was
seen, firstly by the ticket inspector, then by Michaelson in
Badger Lane, where he knew he always took his afternoon
walk around 3.30. His plan of operation was simplicity
itself. He knew it was Burton's day off so he had no

difficulty in entering Hellrake Hall unobserved and
murdering Sir Mortimer Turrett with the heavy brass
snuffer from the lepidoptera room . . .' etc., etc.
Eventually the means, the motive and the opportunity lay
at one suspect's door and the game was over.

To some extent, of course, a version of this game is still
played today, in endless, commonplace television crime
series, but it has lost its flavour. Lumpfish roe has replaced
caviar. The assembly line has replaced the hand-made.
The most popular of bloodsports, as Nicholas Blake a.k.a.
C. Day Lewis, the Poet Laureate, has called it, is dead,
first outlawed by Raymond Chandler and Dashiell
Hammett, and then polished off by Ian Fleming and his
lacklustre imitators. Aston Martins are no substitute for the
three o'clock from Paddington. Science laboratories and
routine cop-shop investigation will never be a match for
the Olympian ratiocination of a Philip Trent or a Roger
Sheringham, Albert Campion or Father Brown. True, the
annual Ruth Rendells and P. D. Jameses still appear,
uneasily attempting to link the new world with the old,
but mostly they are but embalmer's tricks trying to make a
cold corpse life-like.

Roll up your maps of Wiltshire and Norfolk, put away
your flying buttresses and mullioned windows, crumple up
your paste-board homicidal clergy, thespians, ne'er-do-
wells and militia, throw away the family legends and
inherited curses. Farewell God-like Sleuths, we won't be
needing you again in our lifetime. 'All glory passes,' as the
slaves murmured into the ears of the Roman emperors
during triumphal processions.

And so I suspect it will be the same with *me* and my timewarp view of things. I expect, in a maudlin sort of way, that they won't be needing me again in my lifetime.

Perhaps George Devine was right after all in his obsession with experimentation and establishing the right to fail. Lindsay Anderson, a leading Royal Court luminary, once asked me, after *Sleuth* had been on for eight years, 'Have you ever thought of taking it off to make way for newer things?'

'No,' I said. 'I'm establishing the right to succeed!'

Whether or not I *have* succeeded, or whether or not this memoir has succeeded, must be up to you.

After all, you paid for it! And not too much, I hope you're thinking. And if you aren't, if you consider you've been grossly overcharged for a few paltry reminiscences – so what did you expect?

Index

Index

Index